40 Things NOT
to Give up for Lent

A 40 Day Devotional
Guide for Lent

Phil Ressler

Table of Contents

Week of Ash Wednesday:
The Greatest of These

"So now faith, hope, and love abide, these three;
but the greatest of these is love."
(1 Corinthians 13:13, ESV)

1. **Faith** – In what or in whom do you trust? (Matthew 17:20)

2. **Hope** – More than wishful thinking, but a sure confidence. (Hebrews 11:1)

3. **Love** – The greatest. (John 3:16)

4. **Jesus** – He is faithful, provides hope, and is the embodiment of love. (1 John 4:8)

Week 2: Peace

"Peace I leave with you; my peace I give to you. Not as the world gives do I give to you. Let not your hearts be troubled, neither let them be afraid." (John 14:27, ESV)

5. **God's Word** – Heaven and earth may pass away, but God's words never will. (Matthew 24:35)

6. **Gratitude** – It's the antidote to worry, anger, and misery. (1 Thessalonians 5:18)

7. **Patience** – Take a deep breath. (James 5:7)

8. **Rest** – Your value to God is not in your doing, but your being. (Matthew 11:29)

9. **Listening** – When you are talking, you are not listening. (Matthew 7:24)

10. **Silence** – Be still and know that God reigns. (Psalm 46:10)

Week 3: Strength

"I can do all things through him
who strengthens me." (Philippians 4:13, ESV)

11. **Courage** – We are more than conquerors.
     (Romans 8:37)

12. **Persistence** – Good things come to those who
     wait. (Luke 18:7)

13. **Discipline** – It produces freedom.
     (Hebrews 12:11)

14. **Focus** – Single mindedness goes further than
     being scatterbrained. (Hebrews 12:1-2)

15. **Simplicity** – Less is more. (1 Thessalonians 4:11)

16. **Humility** – God lifts up the humble. (James 4:10)

Week 4: Growth

"Rather train yourself for godliness; for while bodily training is of some value, godliness is of value in every way, as it holds promise for the present life and also for the life to come."
(1 Timothy 4:7–8, ESV)

17. **Learning** – There is always something new to learn, no matter how much I master.
(1 Corinthians 13:12)

18. **Discernment** – Not everything you read on the Internet is true. (John 14:6)

19. **New experiences** – Get outside your comfort zone. (2 Corinthians 5:17)

20. **Failure** – Success does not come without failure. (Philippians 3:13-14)

21. **Fitness** – Stewardship of your body (1 Corinthians 16:19)

22. **Vision** – See where you are going. (Ephesians 1:18-19)

Week 5: Relationships

"The glory that you have given me I have given to them, that they may be one even as we are one..."
(John 17:22, ESV)

23. **People** – I can gain the whole world, but if I have no one to share it with . . . (Matthew 16:26)

24. **Grace** – You have been given much. (Colossians 3:12-13)

25. **Forgiveness** – Let it go. (Ephesians 4:32)

26. **Adventure** – Share the ride. (Philippians 4:14)

27. **Respect** – The engine that makes relationships run. (Ephesians 5:21)

28. **Accountability** – One day we all will be held to account. Why not start now? (Romans 14:12)

Week 6: Serving

"But whoever would be great among you must be your servant, and whoever would be first among you must be your slave, even as the Son of Man came not to be served but to serve, and to give his life as a ransom for many."
(Matthew 20:26b–28, ESV)

29. **Compassion** – Seek to understand before being understood. (2 Corinthians 1:3-4)

30. **Prayer** – The world needs it. (1 Timothy 2:1-2)

31. **Generosity** – The more generously you sow, the more you will reap. (2 Corinthians 9:6)

32. **Purpose** – You are still breathing. God has got you here for a reason. (Ephesians 2:10)

33. **Compliments** – No one ever regretted complimenting rather than criticizing. (Colossians 3:16)

34. **Gifts & Abilities** – Don't withhold your blessing from others. (Ephesians 4:11-14)

Holy Week: Commitment

"I appeal to you therefore, brothers, by the mercies of God, to present your bodies as a living sacrifice, holy and acceptable to God, which is your spiritual worship." (Romans 12:1, ESV)

35. **Worship** – God is worthy of all. (Revelation 4:10–11)

36. **Anger** – Fight for what is right. Stand against injustice. (Romans 12:9)

37. **Sacrifice** – No greater love than a man lay down his life. (John 15:13)

38. **Community** – Jesus commands that we love one another as he loves us. (Hebrews 10:25)

39. **Grief** – Even Jesus wept. (2 Corinthians 7:10)

40. **Joy** – It's more than being happy. (Philippians 4:4)

Week 1

Theme for the Week:
The Greatest of These

"So now faith, hope, and love abide, these three;
but the greatest of these is love."
(1 Corinthians 13:13, ESV)

In 1 Corinthians 13:13, we read that there are three that remain. These are faith, hope, and love. 1 Corinthians 13 is known as the great Bible chapter on love. While the chapter is all about love, the Apostle Paul says that faith and hope also remain. As we talk about **40 Things NOT to Give up for Lent**, it would appear that these three (faith, hope, and love) are ideal candidates to top the list. During this first half week of Lent, we will take a deeper look at each. Welcome to the journey.

- **Wednesday:** Faith
- **Thursday:** Hope
- **Friday:** Love
- **Saturday:** Jesus

01.Faith

Ash Wednesday

He (Jesus) said to them, "Because of your little faith. For truly, I say to you, if you have faith like a grain of mustard seed, you will say to this mountain, 'Move from here to there,' and it will move, and nothing will be impossible for you."
(Matthew 17:20, ESV)

Jump

"Jump! You can do it! Daddy will catch you!" I tried to convince my son to jump into the pool. But fear had seized him. He would not do it.

I negotiated some more. I told him I would not let him sink. I talked about the fun he would have. He just needed a little faith.

Then that daring moment came. He screamed. He jumped. He made a splash. I caught him. It was scary. It was thrilling. It was exhilarating.

Almost as soon as he jumped into the water, he was back out of the pool and ready to jump in again. All it took was a little faith, and he was hooked.

Jesus says, 'with a little faith you can move the mountains.' It might seem impossible to move a mountain. There may be many things holding you back from moving a mountain, but at the top of the list is lack of faith. Without faith, it is impossible.

Faith makes possible the impossible. It opens the door to possibility. It was impossible for my son to jump into the pool without faith. As soon as he mustered the faith, it became possible. And he did it! The truth is that you can accomplish so much more when you believe.

Leap Beyond Knowledge and Belief

If we are to jump, it is important to understand the difference between knowledge, belief, and faith. Knowledge, belief, and faith are related, but faith is a leap beyond.

I can have knowledge of God, but not believe in God. You may have knowledge of the Boogie Man, but that does not mean you believe he exists. Many people with knowledge of the Bible don't believe it to be true. Knowledge is foundational for belief, but it does not guarantee belief.

Neither is belief the same as faith. I may believe in God, but that is not the same as trusting in God. I may believe that God exists. I may believe that Jesus died on the cross and rose from the dead. But I still may live in fear. Before he jumped, my son believed I would catch him, but he did not have the faith to take the leap. He was too afraid before he found faith.

Faith has an Object

Faith always has an object. The object of Christian faith is Jesus. It is more than faith in faith itself. Christian faith is more than believing that, if I think happy thoughts, everything is going to be okay.

I trust that Jesus is all I need. I put my life and salvation in his hands. I live obedient to his Word because I trust that God's way is the best way. I am convinced I will not sink because I am convinced he will catch me.

It was not blind optimism that led my son to take the leap. He jumped because he had faith in his dad. His faith had an object. And Jesus desires to be the object of your faith.

Are you ready to jump? Do you believe God will catch you? Faith may seem like a dangerous business. But when you finally jump, you will wonder what you were waiting for. I believe God is inviting you to jump today. What are you waiting for? You can do it. Jump!

Reflection

1. How is faith in God evident in your life? Where do you lack faith?

2. What builds faith?

3. Where is God inviting you to jump? A new business? Asking her to marry you? Volunteering for that leadership position at church?

4. Pray to ask God to increase your faith.

02.Hope

Thursday after Ash Wednesday

*"Now faith is the assurance of things hoped for,
the conviction of things not seen."*
(Hebrews 11:1, ESV)

My First Option or Last Resort?

She came into my office with good intentions. Tears were running down her cheeks. The first thing she said was: "Pastor, I have tried everything. Nothing has worked. I am out of options. So, I am coming to see you."

I am glad she came to see me, but I was disheartened. She had such little confidence in my ability to help that she came to see me last. This has not been a one-time occurrence. Many people will only go to the pastor when all else has failed. We pride ourselves in our ability to help ourselves. We give it our best shot with God as our fallback option.

We have got it backward when we see God as our last resort rather than our #1 option. The order in which we turn to God says much about our hope in God. When we are sick, we go to the doctor. When we are struggling to make ends meet, we look for a job. When our marriage is struggling, we go to the counselor. We often look to human solutions first, and then turn to God when the human solutions don't work. Certainly, God often uses human solutions to help us, but what if we started looking to him first?

Hope vs. Hopefulness

There is a difference between possessing hope and being hopeful. Possessing hope is to be sure and confident. It's more than wishful thinking. The language you use when you talk about God's provision says a lot about your hope. Consider the following responses. Which is the most confident?

1. I hope God will provide for me.

2. I know God will provide for me.

3. God provides for me.

The first statement is hopeful. It is filled with wishful thinking, and is clouded with fear and doubt. The first statement is not going to do much for you.

The second statement is more confident. It looks to the future in faith, but there is still a hint of doubt. You can very easily add a "but" at the end of that statement which will change the whole character of that second statement.

The third statement is certain. God has provided for me in the past. He is providing for me now. And He has the future taken care of. God provides. It's done. There is no need to worry.

Try another one. Consider these statements.

1. I hope God will heal me.
2. I know God will heal me.
3. God is my healer.

Which is hopeful? Which is certain? It is #3. Even though there may be an incurable disease raging in my body, I can still possess hope. I can know that in Christ, every day I am one day closer to my ultimate healing. God is healing me. When I possess hope, I can speak of my future as a present reality. Hope makes real what is not yet.

My Only Option

One of my favorite hymns is "My Hope is Built on Nothing Less." Here are the lyrics of the first verse:

> *My hope is built on nothing less.*
> *Than Jesus' blood and righteousness;*
> *I dare not trust the sweetest frame,*
> *But wholly lean on Jesus' name.*
> *On Christ, the solid Rock, I stand;*
> *All other ground is sinking sand.*

My hope is built on nothing! That is nothing other than the blood of Jesus and his righteousness. In the end, God is not just our first option. He is our only option. There is nothing less (or else) that can save us from death. It's not my works. It's not my money. It's not my religion. One day all the things I know on this earth will fail me. But it doesn't matter because I've got Jesus. He is my hope!

Reflection

1. Do you turn to God first or last?

2. Where do you lack hope? Write out a statement of hope and confidence. Put the statement in a place you will regularly see it.

3. What does hope mean to you?

03.Love

Friday after Ash Wednesday

"For God so loved the world, that he gave his only Son, that whoever believes in him should not perish but have eternal life." (John 3:16, ESV)

The Whole World

God so loved the whole world. It doesn't say he loved some of the world. It doesn't say he loved the Christian world. It doesn't say he loved those who are good and kind in the world. It says that he loved the whole world.

He loves the people you love. He loves your spouse. He loves your kids. He loves your friends. He loves all of those who encourage you and inspire you.

He also loves the people you don't love. He loves the unlovable. He loves the marginalized. He loves that rude and belligerent co-worker. He loves that relative who always takes, but never gives. He loves those who have hurt you in the past. Whatever the barrier that is preventing you from loving another person, God's love conquers that barrier.

We often love the people who have something to offer us in return. On the surface, the starving orphan child in Africa may not have much to offer us. But when we send our support (less than the price of a cup of coffee), it makes us feel good about ourselves. We pat ourselves on the back for being a good person. The orphan child gives us good feelings in return for our love.

It is more difficult to love the person who would do us harm, shows us no appreciation, cuts us off on the parkway, or talks behind our back. Can we love others when there is a cost involved?

Who do you find difficult to love? Recognize this is the measure of God's love for you. You have nothing to offer God in return for his love. He does not love you because you are worthy of his love. In fact, it is just the opposite. You don't deserve God's love, but he loves you anyway.

The Cost of Love

God is love (see 1 John 4:8). He is the embodiment of love. To know love is to know God's love. There are no conditions to God's love. The most selfless act of love ever demonstrated is the gift of Jesus. Jesus died for each and every sinner, not just the sinners that are a little better than the rest.

Love does not look past sin nor accept it. To ignore sin is not loving. We are to speak the truth in love (see Ephesians 4:15). Jesus never had a problem confronting sin.

But neither does God condemn us in our sin (see John 3:17). Instead, he bears our sin. He dies for our sin. He takes our sin upon Himself. There is a cost for our sin, but out of love, he pays the debt that is ours.

If we are to love as God loves, we will not ignore sin. Instead, we will bear the sins of others. There is a sacrifice. There is a cost. We may even be despised for our love. The greatest acts of love are often rejected and chastised.

If we don't know God's love, then we don't know what love is. We can't give away what we don't have. If we don't have God's love, then we can't offer true love. True love is to make God's love known. It is to love as God loved us whatever the cost may be.

Lent is an invitation to immerse ourselves in the love of God. It's an invitation to embrace the cross. It is to allow ourselves to be swept away into God's affection. We see there is no distance God will not go. He doesn't just go the extra mile, he goes all the way. As we are embraced by him, our capacity to embrace others will expand. No sacrifice becomes too great to make known God's love.

Reflection

1. What are the conditions you attach to love?

2. Who do you have difficulty loving? What step can you take to show unconditional love?

3. What does it mean to bear the sin of others?

04.Jesus

Saturday after Ash Wednesday

"Anyone who does not love does not know God, because God is love." (1 John 4:8, ESV)

It might seem strange that Jesus is not at the top of the list. We are four days into this series, and we are now just getting to Jesus. But the truth is that it has all been about Jesus. Jesus is the object of our **faith**, the source or our **hope**, and the definition of **love**. Without Jesus, faith is in vain, hope is baseless, and love is absent.

The Real Jesus

The real Jesus of the Bible is often a different Jesus than the one we envision. We choose the Jesus of our liking. We choose the Jesus who:

— is my best friend.

— invites children to come sit on his lap.

— helps me in times of trouble.

— gives me the inspiration to be all I can be.

— motivates me when I need courage.

Jesus is all of these things, but you need to know he is more. There is the Jesus that comforts us, but there is also the Jesus that confronts us.

Jesus Confronted

When we read the Gospels, Jesus was far more radical and revolutionary than most of us dare to see. His preaching was not always filled with warm fuzzies that made people feel content. He was fiery. He made people squirm. There were many people who praised him. There were also many people who wanted to crucify him.

Jesus confronted sin. He was indignant and rebuked the disciples when they refused to let the little children to come to him (see Mark 10:14). He overturned the tables of the moneychangers in the temple after braiding a whip (see John 2:15-17). He called the Pharisees a "brood of vipers" (see Matthew 12:34). He used imagery of fire and brimstone. He didn't preach that all people would go to heaven, but that some were destined to eternal punishment in hell (see Matthew 5:29-30). Jesus was not always the nice Sunday School Jesus that he is made out to be.

Jesus was divisive. In 1 Peter 2:8, Jesus is described as "a stone of stumbling, and a rock of offense." And Jesus himself said in Luke 12:51: "Do you think that I have come to give peace on earth? No, I tell you, but rather division."

Jesus Challenged

Jesus tells us that if we are to follow him that it means denying ourselves and taking up our cross (see Matthew 16:24). When the rich young man asked Jesus what must he do, Jesus told him to sell all his possession and give it away to the poor (see Luke 18:22). When Peter asked Jesus if he should forgive up to seven times, Jesus said that not just seven times, but 77 times (see Matthew 18:21). Jesus made it clear that it is not easy to follow him, and there is a cost to discipleship.

The Jesus of the Bible will stretch us and challenge us beyond what we believe to be reasonable. More people turned away from following Jesus than followed him. Initially, there were the crowds, but by the end, there was just a handful of followers. Most had deserted him. Most had gone back home. By the time we get to the cross, even his closest friends deserted (see Mark 14:51–52) and denied him (see John 18:27).

Jesus is More

Your relationship with God stands or falls on your relationship with Jesus. Jesus has come that we would know God and live in relationship with God. If you don't know Jesus, you don't know God (see John 14:6).

When we encounter the real Jesus of the Bible, he is more difficult, yet more amazing, all at the same time. I have come to realize that I am more depraved and desperate than I ever realized. The real Jesus confronts my sin in a way that makes me uncomfortable. I am not a good person who needs a little bit of extra help from time to time. I am a beggar with nothing to offer before the Almighty God, deserving only his everlasting punishment.

Still, God's grace is greater than I ever imagined. It reaches further than I could have ever hoped. It meets me where I am. I am more broken, but it is through that brokenness, I discover a fix that is more wonderful than anything else I have ever tried. Jesus is my Savior. He is my all in all.

Reflection

1. How does Jesus most comfort you?

2. How does Jesus most confront you?

3. Pray, asking for Jesus to reveal himself in all his fullness.

Week 2

Theme for the Week: Peace

"Peace I leave with you; my peace I give to you. Not as the world gives do I give to you. Let not your hearts be troubled, neither let them be afraid." (John 14:27, ESV)

Horatio Spafford was a prominent lawyer in Chicago. He was a wealthy man. But in 1871, the Great Chicago fire consumed the city. Spafford lost much of his wealth. In spite of his loss, Spafford would dedicate himself to helping those who had lost everything from the fire.

After two years of serving the needs of those most affected, the Spafford family needed some respite. The family prepared for a vacation to Europe. You could not hop on a plane when traveling to Europe in the 19th century, so the family made plans to make the journey by boat.

Unfortunately, Horatio was delayed by business. But he sent his four daughters and his wife ahead on a ship by the name of Ville du Havre. He would follow on another ship.

On November 22, 1873, while crossing the Atlantic Ocean, the Ville du Havre was struck by another ship. Tragically, 226 people lost their lives, including Horatio's four daughters. His wife, Anna, survived, and upon arriving in England, she sent a telegram back to her husband, "Saved alone."

Spafford boarded the first boat he could find to England to be reunited with his wife. While on the voyage, filled with unimaginable grief, near the place where he lost his daughters, Spafford wrote a poem. You may be familiar with the words.

When peace, like a river, attendeth my way,
When sorrows like sea billows roll
Whatever my lot, Thou hast taught me to say,
It is well, it is well with my soul.
It is well, with my soul,
It is well, it is well with my soul.

Later that poem would be put to music to the tune of "Ville du Havre." We know it today as the beloved hymn: "When Peace Like a River." It is a beautiful hymn, but the significance of the words becomes even more powerful when we know the story behind the song.

After this tragedy, Horatio and Anna Spafford would move to Jerusalem to serve as missionaries to share Christ with the local Muslim and Jewish people. Spafford endured through the darkest hour of his life because of an enduring hope in Jesus.

Peace is not about our circumstances. One thing that is certain is you will have problems in your life. There is not a single person in this world who has their life completely together. Recognizing you have hardships, the question is how you respond to those difficulties. Do you have peace or is your life filled with anxiety and grief?

Peace is about the state of your soul. The world may collapse around you, but you can still have peace when you know Jesus is with you. The peace that God gives to you is the peace that surpasses all understanding (see Philippians 4:7). Jesus says he does not give peace as the world gives peace (see John 14:27). God's peace is a quiet contentment that provides rest for the soul whatever the odds.

In the next week, the first full week in Lent, we will be looking at some of the ways God's peace becomes rooted in our lives so that even in the most difficult times, we might declare it is well, it is well with our souls.

- **Monday:** God's Word
- **Tuesday:** Gratitude
- **Wednesday:** Patience
- **Thursday:** Rest
- **Friday:** Listening
- **Saturday:** Silence

05.God's Word

Week 2: Monday

"Heaven and earth will pass away, but my words will not pass away." (Matthew 24:35, ESV)

Words to Live By

It is said that the pen is mightier than the sword. The point is that words have power. More than you realize! The words you speak and think hold authority. Your words command your life. They may command loss and despair. Or they may command joy and restoration.

So many decisions we make in life are determined by emotions. In turn, our emotions are determined by the way we think. And the way we think is determined by the words we use.

The language we use plays an incredible role in shaping our destiny. If you want to change your future, change your language. We all have words that we live by. These words guide us and direct us. They provide a roadmap to the future. It's called self-fulfilling prophecy.

Everything you say empowers something. You say, "I can't take this." You say, "this is killing me." What do those words create? They create doubt and destructive patterns. They leave you helpless.

Instead, you say, "God can take this." You say, "Jesus has overcome." What do these words create? They create faith. They create optimism. They encourage you to move forward. They are the first steps towards a better day.

What Word?

Where do you get your words? Do your words come from the source of truth or do your words come from some other place? Where do we turn to find worthy words that will bring abundance into our lives?

Peter, the disciple of Jesus, had the answer. He says:

> *"Lord, to whom shall we go? You have the words*
> *of eternal life..." (John 6:68, ESV)*

God's Word is the first and final word. It is the source of our hope. It is God's Word that created the universe, ushered in salvation, and brings all things to fulfillment. This is the importance of God's Word. It is the only Word that stands eternal and is the only Word worth living by:

> *"For it is no empty word for you, but your very*
> *life, and by this word you shall live long..."*
> *(Deuteronomy 32:47, ESV)*

Live It and Declare It?

Our theme for the week is peace. If God's Word is not part of your life, there is a good chance that you lack peace. It is said that a Bible that is worn out is the sign of a person who is not. The opposite is also true.

When it comes to the Word: Read it! Learn it! Memorize it! Study it! Live it! Speak it!

You will not master it overnight. But the more you live in it, a more powerful weapon for good it becomes. When Jesus was tempted by Satan in the desert, he conquered the temptation through declaring the Word (see Matthew 4:1-11). If you lack peace, start declaring God's Word over your life. Let it transform your heart and mind.

Reflection

1. Examine your words. Are you speaking a blessing or a curse over your life?

2. What are some negative thoughts you currently have? What is the opposite truth that God's Word speaks? Write out the truth.

3. Make a commitment to make God's Word part of your daily life. Write down how you will do that. Will it be a Bible reading plan? A memorization challenge? Or a study?

06.Gratitude

Week 2: Tuesday

*"Give thanks in all circumstances; for this
is the will of God in Christ Jesus for you."
(1 Thessalonians 5:18, ESV)*

Thanksgiving comes around once a year. It is a time to gather together with family. We watch some football and eat a nice meal. While the day is supposed to be about giving thanks, the actual practice of giving thanks is often neglected.

The Apostle Paul says to give thanks in all circumstances. In other words, gratitude is something to be practiced every day. It is not something to be reserved for one day of the year at the end of November.

But instead of practicing gratitude, it is often easier to count all the things that are not right in life. However, when we engage in an intentional discipline of giving thanks, good things begin to happen. Here is a list of some of the benefits of gratitude:

Gratitude creates joy

It is better to count your blessings than it is to wallow in your shortcomings. When you practice gratitude, you realize that life is not as bad as it might seem. You begin to see that life may be better than you perceive. Satan wants to rob your life of joy, and will work overtime to make you blind to the blessings God has granted. Gratitude will help you see the good things.

Gratitude saves you money

Gratitude builds contentment. When you have contentment, you will not feel the need to buy that latest and greatest gadget with money you don't have. The goal of advertising is to make you feel discontent with your life and convince you that buying the latest and greatest is the key to your happiness. But if you are already happy, you will realize you do not need it.

Gratitude creates hope

When you practice gratitude, you will see you have much more in your favor than you realize. You will start to recognize the gifts God has given you to make a difference. You will begin to see God's ability to empower you for more. Too often, people lack trust in God's ability to prosper them. But gratitude will work to conquer the fear of failure.

Gratitude opens up opportunity

As gratitude opens your eyes to see the world in a new way, you will begin to see new opportunities. Opportunities present themselves to those who have the eyes to see them. It's not that you don't have opportunities. It is that you don't have the eyes to see them. As we are more attentive to God's work in our lives, we will see things we did not see before.

Gratitude creates healthy relationships

We can easily take the people in our lives for granted. It might be our spouse, volunteers at church, or the waiter at the restaurant. We all enjoy being appreciated. We all relish when other people take notice of what we are doing. And other people will appreciate when you offer them gratitude. Expressing gratitude towards others can do amazing things in your relationships.

To whom can you express gratitude? To whom can you show appreciation? Write a note. Send a message. Tell them in person. Let them know your appreciation. It will be a blessing to them. It will be a blessing to you. It will be a blessing to your relationship. It will be a blessing to God.

Reflection.

1. Make a list of the things for which you are grateful.

2. Create a gratitude journal to keep each day.

3. Write some thank you notes to people you appreciate.

07.Patience

Week 2: Wednesday

"Be patient, therefore, brothers, until the coming of the Lord. See how the farmer waits for the precious fruit of the earth, being patient about it, until it receives the early and the late rains."
(James 5:7, ESV)

Recently, I was enjoying a daddy-daughter date night. The date consisted of a trip to an indoor amusement park. We chose indoors because it was a cold night. So, when we arrived, we checked our coats at the coat check.

As we were preparing to leave the park, we went to retrieve our coats. There was one lady who was checking out. We took our place in line behind her and waited while the transaction was completed. Just as this lady was finishing, another lady jumped in front of us. I don't think it was intentional. She seemed out of sorts and extremely disconcerted. You could see the stress and anxiety oozing out of her.

My first thoughts were: "Lady, who do you think you are?" I felt the urge to loudly say, "excuse me!" But in a split second, I thought better. I said to myself, "let it go. What is the hurry?" Here I was spending time with my daughter, and this inconvenience would be the opportunity to spend a few more moments together. We had nowhere we needed to be. To make a big scene would not benefit anyone.

What is the rush?

Life passes by so quickly. But we are always in such a hurry to get somewhere. Life is not so much about the destination. It's about the journey. Enjoy the ride. Enjoy each moment for what it is.

I remember as a kid that I could not wait for Christmas to come. But more often than not, the anticipation of Christmas was so much more exciting than Christmas itself. I can think about so many memories surrounding Christmas. So many of those memories are not about Christmas Day, but about the days leading up to Christmas. Why was I in such a rush for Christmas to arrive?

Think back to your past. Think of the moments you wish you could get back. Maybe it is time with the kids when they were little. Maybe it is time with a loved one that is no longer with us. In the same way, one day you will wish to have this present time back. So, allow yourself to linger in the moment now.

See the opportunity through inconvenience

When you are inconvenienced, consider the opportunity that might be presenting itself. The extra time in the coat check line was some extra time to spend with my daughter. Getting caught in that traffic jam is a few more minutes to enjoy an audiobook in the car. Getting stuck in the line at the grocery store is potentially an opportunity to make a new friend with the person in line next to you. Losing the internet connection on your phone is an opportunity to look up from the screen to see the amazing creation around you. Sometimes that interruption is a gentle nudging by God to experience something greater.

Instant anything is rarely better than the real deal. Instant may be convenient, but never as sweet. A slow and home-cooked meal is always better than fast food. What you lose in quick, you gain in quality. The challenge for you is to focus on what you gain rather than what you lose when you are inconvenienced.

Intentionally practice patience

I live just outside Manhattan. When we take trips into the city, I enjoy people watching. Just grab a bench in Bryant Park and watch the people walk by. One word that describes Manhattan is busy. There is so much that is happening all at once. Maybe nothing gives me more of a sense of peace than being in the middle of the busyness with nowhere to be and nothing to accomplish.

So many of us are so focused on what we are doing, that we fail to notice everything around us. Be present in the moment. Look for ways you can slow down, so you can start to see inconveniences as blessings rather than curses.

Reflection

1. Where do you find impatience in your life?

2. How do you intentionally practice patience?

3. What inconveniences in your life became blessings in disguise?

08.Rest

Week 2: Thursday

"Take my yoke upon you, and learn from me, for I am gentle and lowly in heart, and you will find rest for your souls." (Matthew 11:29, ESV)

The wind and the waves were tossing the boat around. Where was Jesus? He was sleeping (see Mark 4:35-41). How could Jesus be sleeping at a moment like this? The boat was sinking. This was not the moment to sleep.

A lot of us feel like we can't get rest. There is never a good moment to take a nap. We are running all day long. We go to bed late and get up early. Even our days off are not truly days off. Work, work, and more work! There is always work to be done. How can you sleep at a moment like this?

God gives the Sabbath

But we need rest. When God created the universe, he rested on the seventh day (see Genesis 2:1-3). As part of the order of creation, he gave us the gift of the Sabbath Day. To remind us of this gift, he gave us the third commandment: "Remember the Sabbath Day, to keep it holy." (Exodus 20:8, ESV)

God created you, and he knows better about how you were designed to work than you do. It's good to listen to your designer. And he says that you need rest. Sometimes, the most spiritually beneficial thing we can do is take a nap.

Work from your rest

When Jesus lived, the workday began at sunset. This is different from the way we approach the day. We view the day beginning when the sun rises in the morning. That is the start of the day, and when the day starts, it is time to get to work.

But when the day begins at sunset, the first thing to do is rest. We go to sleep. As we rest, we put all the tasks on our to-do list into God's hands while we take the time to be renewed and refreshed. Rest requires a trust that God will give us everything we need to complete our work. Instead of resting from our work, we work from our rest.

A lack of rest is a lack of faith

Why can't you get rest? Why do you have so much anxiety that prevents you from sleeping? There is a good chance that you are having a hard time giving the things in your life over to God. Instead of living by faith, you are trying to control everything.

God gave us 24 hours in a day. He gave us seven days in the week. God knows what he is doing. He gave us exactly the right amount of time to get done everything he has called us to do. If we don't have enough time to get everything done; there is a good chance we are doing more than we were created to do. It's time to loosen your grip on some of the stuff you are holding on to so tight.

You are more important than your work

Finally, don't define yourself by your work. You are not valuable to God because of what you do, but because of who God made you to be. Your value is in who you are in Christ. You don't have to prove anything to God. Jesus has already proved everything necessary.

You can rest content, knowing God will provide. The work that you think is so important will still be there tomorrow. And even if you are to complete the work today, it will just mean that there will be new tasks to be accomplished tomorrow. There will always be work to be done, so get your rest.

Reflection

1. Take a nap.

2. Do you have a hard time finding rest? Why?

3. What can you do to prioritize rest in your life?

09.Listening

Week 2: Friday

"Everyone then who hears these words of mine and does them will be like a wise man who built his house on the rock." (Matthew 7:24, ESV)

Seek to understand

We live in a time where there is a charged political atmosphere. There are strong opinions. But the problem is not the strong opinions. The problem is that we always have something to say, but rarely hear what is being said.

We want to be understood. We want to make our point. We want others to empathize with us. We want others to approve of what we believe. So we are always looking for the angle to make our point known. We insist on proving we are right.

The point is that we are good at talking. We are not as good at listening. But what if we sought to understand more than we sought to be understood? Instead of plotting to make our point known, we would work to comprehend another person's position? If this happened, it would go a long way towards unity not only in politics, but also in marriages, churches, and places of work.

The irony is that those who seek to hear are often the ones who are best heard. When you actively listen to others, it will encourage others to respect you and your opinion. They respect what you have to say because you respect what they have to say. They will listen to you.

Seek to hear God

How much more does the principle of listening apply to our relationship with God? Jesus tells us that the person who listens to God's Word is wise. Our prayers are often talking at God rather than talking with God. We will go out of our way to make our troubles known to God. But we don't have the same urgency to hear what God has to say about those troubles.

God is constantly speaking. He is constantly making his presence known. If you don't hear God speak, it is not because God is not speaking. The problem is that we are not listening. You are not actively seeking God's gentle whispers.

God's voice can be heard, but it is subtle. It does not scream out at us. If you are looking for God to reveal himself through a bolt of lightning or an earthquake, you are probably not going to hear his voice. He doesn't put billboards up along the roadside.

Seeking God's voice is seeking it where it is found. It is found in opening the pages of the Scriptures. It is found in times of quiet. It is found when we disconnect from our phones, our TV's, and computers. It is found in Jesus.

As you hear from God, examine your words and your actions in light of what he is speaking. When we live disobedient to God's Word, it hinders our ability to hear from God. The more we align ourselves with God's revealed Word, the easier it becomes to hear further revelation. God is speaking. Do you have the ears to hear?

Reflection

1. How do you intentionally listen to God?

2. In your next conversation, let go of the desire to make your point, and simply understand the other person's perspective.

3. Are you living obedient to God's voice? How does disobedience hinder your ability to hear?

10.Silence

Week 2: Saturday

"Be still, and know that I am God. I will be exalted among the nations, I will be exalted in the earth!"
(Psalm 46:10, ESV)

Music is a big part of worship at our church. A few weeks back, we planned a service without any music. It was different. It was even uncomfortable at times. Singing songs on Sunday morning is what we know and what we are comfortable with. We like to make a joyful noise unto God. But have you ever considered making joyful silence?

Sometimes the greatest act of worship is not to sing a song, but to simply be still. When you visit the Grand Canyon, it is a religious experience. You stand over the edge of the canyon, and you are overwhelmed by its size and beauty. It brings you to a place where you recognize how small you are, and that you are part of a creation that is much bigger. As you stand at the edge, you don't sing a song to the Grand Canyon about how great it is. You stand there in silence and awe. You are amazed. There are no words.

We need more silence. We live in a noisy world. When was the last time you experienced silence? Do you ever find yourself turning on the TV or the radio at home simply to have noise? The silence can be uncomfortable. We create noise, so we are more comfortable.

We are so constantly surrounded by noise that we have grown immune to it. We don't even hear the noise around us. When we encounter silence, it is deafening. Silence is life-altering.

In Psalm 46:10, it says to be still and to know God. What does that say about our noisy lifestyles? How can you intentionally practice silence and stillness?

Reflection

Take the next 10 minutes just to be still. Don't do anything. Eliminate as much noise around you as possible. Consider what you hear in the silence.

Week 3

Theme for the Week: Strength

"I can do all things through him who strengthens me." (Philippians 4:13, ESV)

Our theme for the week is strength. There is physical strength, but there is also strength of character. Strength gives us the ability to endure and accomplish more. In difficult times, we call upon God's strength to push through. Strength gives us the ability to aim higher and run farther.

The source of our greatest strength is not found in ourselves. It is found in Jesus. We are reminded in Philippians 4:13 that we can do all things through Christ who gives us strength. If we rely on our strength, we will not get far.

Human strength is fleeting. It runs out. You may be physically strong today, but one day, age or illness will take that strength from you.

Human strength is also limited. Eventually, you will encounter forces that are stronger than yourself. You may be strong, but there is always something or someone who is stronger.

But God's strength endures. God's strength is always replenished. And there is no force in the universe that is stronger. There is nothing that stands against God's strength. So, if we are to find true strength, it will be God's strength.

This week we will look into how we tap into God's strength:

— **Monday:** Courage

— **Tuesday:** Persistence

— **Wednesday:** Discipline

— **Thursday:** Focus

— **Friday:** Simplicity

— **Saturday:** Humility

11.Courage

Week 3: Monday

"No, in all these things we are more than conquerors through him who loved us."
(Romans 8:37, ESV)

You are not a conqueror. You are MORE than a conqueror! In Christ, you are stronger and more able than you ever realize.

But too often, we feel like victims. We are defeated by the words of others. Or we are physically defeated by an illness. There are forces in this world that knock us down. They seemingly overpower us.

How can I be MORE than a conqueror when I am knocked down? It is called courage. There are many people who fail to experience abundant life because they don't have the courage to get up after being knocked down. They take on the role of victim.

When you have God on your side, you may get punched and knocked down, but that does not mean you will get knocked out. There are many things in this world that can put us down, but there is nothing that can keep us down. Courage is to face danger, hardship, or uncertainty, knowing the victory is already won. You are not a victim. You have more power to control your circumstances than you realize.

There is no greater example of this than the death and resurrection of Jesus. On Good Friday, he was put down in the grave. Death had seemingly won. It was a dark day. But the grave could not keep him. On Easter Sunday, he would rise up. He defeated death and the grave through the resurrection. Now the saying is true:

> *"Death is swallowed up in victory. O death, where is your victory? O death, where is your sting?"*
> *(1 Corinthians 15:54-55, ESV)*

If you are a believer, the same Spirit that raised Jesus from the dead is at work in you (see Romans 8:11). Rise up! God has given you the ability to rise up against whatever odds you face. If he can defeat death, he can defeat whatever it is that stands against you. Stand up on your two feet. Refuse to be defeated.

You might be afraid. That is okay. Courage is not the absence of fear. It is the ability to get up in spite of our fears. The source of our courage is Christ and the victory won through the resurrection. While this world may take my life, it cannot take my salvation.

Reflection

1. Where do you allow yourself to play the role of victim?

2. Where is Christ calling you to stand in courage and faith?

3. How do you build courage?

12.Persistence

Week 3: Tuesday

"And will not God give justice to his elect, who cry to him day and night? Will he delay long over them?" (Luke 18:7, ESV)

The widow comes to the judge. She asks for justice, but the judge refuses to grant her request. But the widow does not give up. She does not take "no" for an answer. She goes back to the judge. Then, she goes back to the judge again, and then again. Finally, she wears the judge down. The judge says to himself, "though I neither fear God nor respect man, yet because this widow keeps bothering me, I will give her justice, so that she will not beat me down by her continual coming." (Luke 18:4-5, ESV)

The widow was eventually granted justice through her persistence. She endured. She wore the judge out with her constant nagging.

One and Done

There have been times when someone has come to me and told me that they prayed to God, and that God did not answer their prayer. My response was, "how do you know that God did not answer your prayer?"

We come to God and say a prayer. Then, God does not answer us in the timeframe we expect. So, we conclude prayer did not work. Nothing happened. So, we give up on God. We are "one-and-done."

I find it interesting how quick we are to give up on prayer. We have the mindset to offer a single prayer, thinking the work is done. We expect the magic to happen. But often, the answer to our prayer is found in the waiting for God's response.

In the Sermon on the Mount, Jesus says:

> *"But seek first the kingdom of God and his righteousness, and all these things will be added to you." (Matthew 6:33, ESV)*

The sense of this verse is not just to seek once, but to keep on seeking. Seek first, second, third, and fourth the kingdom of God. It is to seek the kingdom above all else. Don't even consider seeking anything else, until you discover the kingdom. Be persistent.

Nagging God

On the opposite extreme of "one-and-done" are the people who have come to me, and are worried about nagging God. They are fearful that God is tired of hearing their prayers and pleas. They don't want to be a bother to God.

But God does not grow tired of your prayer. He desires your prayer. He wants you to come to him. It's all about the relationship. He wants to know you and to be known by you. God has a great big universe to support and nurture. But he also desires to take care of you. Nothing is too great for him to do. And nothing is too small to ask of him.

Reflection

1. Where do you need to be more persistent in your prayer life?

2. What is the benefit of persistence?

3. How does waiting on God enrich us?

13.Discipline

Week 3: Wednesday

"For the moment all discipline seems painful rather than pleasant, but later it yields the peaceful fruit of righteousness to those who have been trained by it." (Hebrews 12:11, ESV)

Discipline is often viewed as a dirty word. It is seen as a bad thing. But in Hebrews 11, it says, that while discipline can be painful, it produces the peaceful fruit of righteousness.

At its heart, discipline means to instruct. It's related to the word disciple. A disciple is one who is instructed by a teacher. And we are all called to be disciples of Jesus. Discipline is not all bad. In fact, it is quite good.

Sometimes discipline is enforced through a negative consequence to bad behavior. At other times, discipline is to set aside what I want to do at a given moment for something better at a later time. This latter type of discipline brings about freedom.

Pay Now and Play Later

John Maxwell says, "You can pay now and play later, OR you can play now and pay later. Either way you have to pay." The point is that there are consequences to our actions. We can do whatever we want at a given moment. We can live disciplined, or we can live undisciplined. But we will reap what we sow.

I spent last week in Haiti. We stayed at the Mission of Hope, Haiti. Mission of Hope is located in a beautiful area of Haiti. It is situated in the foothills to the mountains, overlooking the Caribbean Sea.

One day, I got up at 5:00 am to go for a 3-mile run. My discipline is to run every other day, regardless of the weather. But on this day, the weather was gorgeous. The view was amazing with the sun rising over the mountains. It was all worth it to be up at 5:00 am. The scenery made me almost forget about how hard it was to run up the side of mountain. I didn't need any motivation for this run. It was something to which I looked forward.

Then, I came home to New Jersey. We were welcomed to four inches of snow after experiencing 80 and 90-degree temperatures in Haiti. But I was going to stick with my running discipline. The view from the treadmill was not nearly as inspiring as the sunrise coming over the mountains of Haiti. I certainly did not have the motivation as I did before. But I still ran. I stuck with the discipline.

What enabled me to pursue my discipline was to "know my why." I was not going to enjoy the run on the treadmill but knew I would enjoy the result of the run.

It was not about what I wanted at the moment. At that moment, I did not want to get on the treadmill. My motivation was about what I want tomorrow and into the future. It was the sense of accomplishment. It was that my fitness gives me the ability to keep up with my young children. It is that I want to be around for them for a long time, and enjoy my grandchildren. It is knowing my "why" that gives me the motivation to stick with my discipline and live as healthy as I can, even if that means getting on the treadmill when I don't want.

Discipline Brings Freedom

Discipline is ultimately about freedom. I discipline myself to practice spiritual disciplines to allow me to experience a deeper and more intimate relationship with God. I discipline myself to live on less than I earn to allow me to experience freedom from debt and worry about money. I discipline myself to work in spite of the many distractions to accomplish more, and enjoy my free time without the nagging thoughts about unfinished work. For many, discipline is only about restricting my choices. But for those who are trained by discipline, it opens a world of possibilities.

Reflection

1. Where do you lack discipline?

2. How can you develop greater discipline in your life?

3. What does discipline make possible in your life?

14.Focus

Week 3: Thursday

"Therefore, since we are surrounded by so great a cloud of witnesses, let us also lay aside every weight, and sin which clings so closely, and let us run with endurance the race that is set before us, looking to Jesus, the founder and perfecter of our faith, who for the joy that was set before him endured the cross, despising the shame, and is seated at the right hand of the throne of God."
(Hebrews 12:1–2, ESV)

F.O.C.U.S

What is focus? Here is a great acronym:

- **F** - follow
- **O** - one
- **C** - course
- **U** - until
- **S** - success

I am such a scatterbrain. I am all over the place. I have got a million things running through my mind all the time. I am constantly switching back and forth from one task to the next. Focus is one of those things with which I struggle. Too often, I am following multiple courses, and fail to experience success in any one because I am trying to do too many things. One task is left unfinished while I am already taking on a new task.

The Myth of Multi-tasking

There is a myth called multi-tasking. Studies show we don't multi-task. We switch from one thing to the next really fast. Our minds can only focus on one thing at a time. We have become so efficient at moving back and forth between things that it seems as if we are doing more than one thing at a time. But we are still only doing one thing at a time.

God did not make you to multi-task. He gives you each and every moment for what it is. There is peace when you are doing the one thing God intends for you to do at a given moment.

Be Fully Present

As I said, this is one of my great struggles. I am at home, but my mind is at work. And there are times when I am at work, but my mind is at home. The challenge is to be fully present in the moment. When at home, to be at home. When at work, to be at work. Your body can be present in one place, but your mind can be elsewhere.

You may not even realize how distracted you are. There are weapons of mass distraction all around us. Focus is not so much about that which we say "yes;" it is about that which we say "no." When I am doing my morning devotion, I say no to everything else. My sole focus is on Jesus. My focus is on him because I have eliminated other distractions.

In today's verse, the author of Hebrews encourages us to throw off every weight and sin that clings to us. He talks about running with endurance the race marked before us. Our focus is Jesus. He is the one who resolutely focused on the cross and our salvation. His resolute focus enabled him to accomplish the greatest mission in the history of the world.

Reflection

1. Where do you struggle with a lack of focus? What are the weapons of mass distraction that most affect you?

2. Do you have time in your day when your sole focus is on Jesus?

3. Do one thing for the next 45 minutes. Eliminate all other distractions.

15.Simplicity

Week 3: Friday

"And to aspire to live quietly, and to mind your own affairs, and to work with your hands, as we instructed you..." (1 Thessalonians 4:11, ESV)

A few days ago, I shared how I had taken a recent trip to Haiti. One day on this trip, we drove up and into the mountains.

From where we were staying, it was an hour–long ride. It was not a pleasant experience, riding on the bumpy gravel roads. It seemed like the drive went on and on. We so eagerly anticipated being done with the drive, and for the bouncing to end.

But we continued to drive and drive. There was no sign of civilization except for a random person here and there walking down the mountain. The question had to be asked. From where did they come? How far did they walk? How long would it take them to walk down the mountain?

The answer was that these people came from a village deep in the mountains. They had walked for many miles, and it might take all day to finish their journey.

Life is different there. It is simpler. If all that person was to do on this day was to walk down the mountain, then that is all they do on that day.

As Americans, we could not grasp spending the whole day walking down the mountain. We had so much to do. We were focused on efficiency. We used a car to get where we were going as quickly as possible. It would still take us an hour. We would make our visit and drive back down the mountain, passing the same person we passed on the way up. Next, we would grab our lunch. After lunch, we were off to our afternoon activities. There was so much we had to get done that we didn't have the time to spend the day walking down the mountain.

It is a different mindset. One of the Haitian Nationals that we work with once told me, "You've got the watch, and I've got the time." We don't have time, because of the busy and complicated lives we live.

Sometimes we might desire a simpler life. We complain about how much we have to do. But here is a truth: You agreed to do everything you are now doing. You put everything that is on your calendar on your calendar. You put everything that is on your to-do list on your to-do list. You agreed to it all. At some point in time, you said yes.

No one is forcing you right now to say yes to everything you have said yes to. Your life does not need to be as complicated as you have made it be. You may need to make some difficult choices. But you can live a simpler life.

We have all these tools and technologies that are designed to simplify our lives. But instead of using the tools to more effectively get our work done so that we can enjoy the other parts of life, we use these tools to work more. A car enables us to travel more places, so we add more to our agenda. A cell phone allows us to check email more often, so we send more messages. Just because we can do more things, does not mean we should do more things. The tools to simplify our lives become tools to complicate our lives.

Consider the words from 1 Thessalonians 4:11. Aspire to live a quiet life. What does that mean to you? Instead of doing it all, how can you simplify to do what is most important?

Reflection

1. How have you unnecessarily complicated your life? What are the things you can let go of?

2. What tools intended to simplify your life have complicated your life?

3. What do you think it means to live a quiet life?

16.Humility

Week 3: Saturday

"Humble yourselves before the Lord, and he will exalt you." (James 4:10, ESV)

Yes, you can! You can be whatever you want to be. If you set your mind to it, nothing is impossible. This is the mantra we hear. These are lessons we instill in our children. But as we enter into adulthood, we settle for something less. We allow mediocrity to become the default.

As I write this, my dream of becoming professional ball player has come and gone. I have now reached the age where every player in Major League Baseball is younger than I am. Instead of aspiring to what I could be, I am now reflecting on what could have been. As much as I aspire to accomplish this dream, it is not going to happen. I have accepted it.

There is a bit of humility to recognize that it is not happening. Humility is a good thing. James tells us if we humble ourselves before the Lord, that he will lift you up. Humility is to recognize that you are not everything you think you are or want to be. Humility helps you to see yourself for who you are. Humility helps you:

See what is possible

While it might not be possible for you to accomplish one dream, God has given you some other great things to aspire towards. Humility will give you the eyes to see other doors that God may be opening up. Instead of setting your heart so much on what you want, set your heart on what God wants. Sometimes having your heart so set on your dream may blind you to God's dream for you.

Ask for help

We don't like to ask for help. One of the most popular sections in the book store is the self-help section. We pride ourselves on being self-made. Admitting that we need help can be terribly difficult. But if you could have solved your problem on your own, you would have already done it. The reason that so many of us are held back from the abundance God wants to pour into our lives is that we have not humbled ourselves to ask for help.

Admit you are wrong

There are times when you stay on a course because you don't want to admit you are wrong. We are stubborn. We would rather die on our hill than to get down off of it. We think that admitting we were wrong is to admit that we are inferior.

Many people find it difficult to examine their faith. They find it hard to ask the difficult questions. I believe the reason for that is a fear that we might discover that our faith has been misplaced. But if you are confident that your faith is in the truth, there should be no reason why you would not want to examine it. And if your faith is misplaced, are you not better off letting go of it to walk in the truth? The point is don't be afraid to be wrong.

Be teachable

No matter how much talent and ability I have, no matter how much experience I acquire, there is always something to learn. The thing that often separates the professional from the amateur is being teachable. The moment you become complacent is the moment an industry passes you by. Humility is to recognize that you may be gifted, and that God has tremendously blessed you in a certain area, but that you still have room to grow.

Reflection

1. Where do you need to ask for help?

2. Where do you need to admit you are wrong?

3. Where do you have room to grow?

Week 4

Theme for the Week: Growth

"Rather train yourself for godliness; for while bodily training is of some value, godliness is of value in every way, as it holds promise for the present life and also for the life to come."
(1 Timothy 4:7–8, ESV)

Learning from experience

When I started college, I went to Knox College in Galesburg, IL. When I shared this with people, more than a few people sarcastically responded that they had gone to the school of "hard knox." There is something to be said for experience.

I wish I knew 20 years ago what I know today. Life would have been much easier. But it took 20 years of experience and learning to get to the point I am today. I have grown in so many ways. I needed those 20 years of experience.

Life experiences teach us so much. I can relate to those who sarcastically responded to me. I recognize that I have learned so much more from the school of "hard knocks" than I ever learned in school. I am sure you have too.

You will not stay where you are

You are either growing stronger in your faith, or you are growing weaker in your faith. You are either growing closer to your spouse, or you are drifting apart. You are either living life more abundantly, or you are experiencing greater scarcity.

God wants you to experience growth. He desires you win at life. He wants you to experience a fuller more abundant life (see John 10:10). He wants for your tomorrow to be even better than today.

This happens through discipleship and stewardship. It is said that you learn from your mistakes or you learn from the mistakes of others. Either way, you learn. It is from the school of "hard knocks" (learning from our mistakes) or the school of wisdom (learning from the mistakes of others) that we grow.

This week, we will talk about the growth that comes through discipleship and stewardship. These are the six things we will look at this week:

- **Monday:** Learning
- **Tuesday:** Discernment
- **Wednesday:** New experiences
- **Thursday:** Failure
- **Friday:** Fitness
- **Saturday:** Vision

17.Learning

Week 4: Monday

"For now we see in a mirror dimly, but then face to face. Now I know in part; then I shall know fully, even as I have been fully known."
(1 Corinthians 13:12, ESV)

For now we see dimly in a mirror. We don't know what we don't know. I am no rocket scientist. I don't even know the first thing about rocket science. I am so ignorant about rocket science that I no knowledge of the things I have not learned. I don't know even the first thing I would need to learn. As I would start to learn the basics, I would soon discover that there is so much more to this science than I ever imagined.

They say that ignorance is bliss. I am not sure how true that is. The first step in growth and overcoming life challenges is to recognize there are things you don't know. It is a miserable life to think you know it all, and then wonder why you are struggling in so many ways. Being teachable is the first step towards growth and overcoming the challenges we face.

Be Curious

When we were little, we asked so many questions. We asked why the sky is blue. We asked why the grass is green. We probably wore our parents out with our questions. But somewhere along the way, we lost the curiosity. We stopped asking the questions. But it is through asking questions that we grow in faith and knowledge. Don't be afraid to ask questions about God and faith. He is a big God and is bigger than any question you might ask. Don't hesitate to ask the hard questions.

Seek Knowledge

When you ask the question, seek knowledge. Seek to understand. God's creation is amazing. And the more you learn, the more equipped you will be to experience God's abundance. God created you to win at life. God wants you to experience abundance in every part of your life.

I have found that there is no better way to acquire knowledge than by reading. Not reading Facebook or blog posts but reading books. There is something to be said for long form reading. We live in a soundbite, quote, and cliché world. We often lack depth in understanding and wisdom. Reading books helps us to achieve a depth of knowledge.

But don't stop there. There are so many ways in our modern world to acquire knowledge. There is no area of your life where you cannot find a book, a video, or podcast on the subject. There have been so many repairs I have made in my home by watching YouTube videos. These instructional videos have literally saved me thousands of dollars in repair costs.

Apply knowledge

Maybe the most important thing that we can do is apply the knowledge we learn. King Solomon said:

> *"My son, beware of anything beyond these. Of making many books there is no end, and much study is a weariness of the flesh."*
> *(Ecclesiastes 12:12, ESV)*

Sometimes the last thing we need is to read another book or participate in another Bible study. We haven't taken what we learned in the last one and applied the knowledge. Being filled with facts and knowledge does us no good unless we put it to work.

One of the things that I work hard to do after I finish reading a book is to write down my top 10 take-a-ways from the book. After I write down my take-a-ways, I write down three things I will do differently having this new knowledge. Then, I seek to do them.

Reflection
1. What is one skill or discipline that you are currently focused on learning?

2. What is the last non-fiction book you read? What were your top three take-a-ways? Have you put anything into practice from your reading?

3. Why do you think learning is an important lifelong skill?

18.Discernment

Week 4: Tuesday

Jesus said to him, "I am the way, and the truth, and the life. No one comes to the Father except through me." (John 14:6, ESV)

The Battle for the Truth

The truth! Not everything you read on the Internet is true. I hope you know that. We've learned about this new thing called "Fake News." But it's not a new thing. There has always been "Fake News." The "True News" is something that has been convoluted, manipulated, and outright assaulted since the beginning of time.

It started in the Garden of Eden. Satan took the truth about the Tree of the Knowledge of Good and Evil, and twisted as a means to his own end. He was "crafty" in devising a scheme. Adam and Eve were deceived, and it led to sin entering into the world (see Genesis 3:1-13).

It's disappointing to see believers fail to exercise discernment when it comes to the truth. It compromises our witness in regard to the real truth. The next time you prepare to click "share" on your

Facebook account check, double check, and triple check if what you are sharing is indeed true. The next time you are about to exaggerate about one of your accomplishments, bite your lip. Exercise the truth that God has entrusted to you. It is better not to share than to share something which is false or misleading.

Satan is described as the Father of Lies (see John 8:44). In Ephesians 6, we are told to put on the full armor of God against the devil and his schemes, and that we will be able to stand. Realize there is a battle for the truth. The very first thing we are told to put on before anything else is the belt of truth (see Ephesians 6:14). There is a reason the belt of truth is listed first. If we don't have the truth, all the other armor will be useless. We will fall without the truth.

If we don't have the truth, what do we really have? There is one truth, and he has a name. He is Jesus! He is the way! The only way! And the truth! Nothing but the truth! And as we live in the truth, we will experience abundant life! When we fail to walk in the truth, we are left in a world of hurt.

The Truth about You

The starting point of discernment is discerning your relationship with God and your standing with him. I find so many people struggle in life because they fail to discern God's word of truth about who they are. They have failed to grasp that they are a child of God. They think that they've got to work, earn, or do something to win God's love. God does not love you because of what you do. He loves you because of who he made you to be in Christ.

When we fail to embrace the truth, we are vulnerable to the lies of the culture that tell us we need to make more money, be more beautiful, buy the latest gadget, or have a greater following. The truth is that God made you who he made you to be, and you are loved and special in his eyes. There is nothing more you need to be.

Right thinking leads to right living. Wrong thinking leads to wrong living. If we misunderstand the most important relationship we have in life (our relationship with God), we are going to fail to get much else right. It's like a domino effect. Discern the truth!

Reflection

1. When was a time you failed to discern the truth and got burned?

2. How can you be more discerning of the truth?

3. What are three deeply held untruths you can't let go about your relationship with God?

19.New Experiences

Week 4: Wednesday

"Therefore, if anyone is in Christ, he is a new creation. The old has passed away; behold, the new has come." (2 Corinthians 5:17, ESV)

I grew up in the Midwest United States. The first time I ever traveled outside of the Midwest was the summer I graduated from high school when our church youth group took a trip to New Orleans for a National Youth Gathering. When I went to college, over two hours from home, it seemed like I would be living on the other side of the world. The first time I flew on an airplane was when I played on my college baseball team. I had very limited travel experience. You might say I was sheltered.

When I was in seminary, I chose to study in Israel for a summer. This was an overwhelming experience, but it was so fulfilling. It was beyond anything this Midwestern boy ever thought he would do. I would travel by myself and live in a foreign country for several months. It was scary great. When I arrived, I discovered that most of my apprehensions about going on this trip were unfounded. It was one of the best experiences of my life, and I was better for it. My biggest regret was that I had not planned to stay longer, and that I had not done it sooner.

Another experience was trying sushi for the first time. I could not fathom eating raw fish. But now it is one of my favorite lunch appointments with one of our deacons at our church. I would never have learned how much I like sushi if I had not stepped out of my comfort zone.

There is a reluctance that many of us have to the new and the unknown. We are comfortable with what we know. We make assumptions about the unknown that often have little to do with reality. Whether it's trying a new food, traveling to a new place, joining a new group, or volunteering for new activity; it can make us anxious.

Two days ago, I shared that we don't know what we don't know. The unknown is the unknown. You never know what God has in store. We often fear the worst when it comes to the unknown, but more often than not, the unknown brings unexpected and wonderful surprises. The unknown is more than we ever imagined.

You may not realize what brings you the most joy and fulfillment. The more I open myself to new experiences, the more my tastes and my desires change. There is a more beautiful and wonderful world out there than I know from my limited experience. I've come to realize that there are things that I like even more than the things that I think I like. If only I would try them. God is about new starts, new beginnings, and new experiences. Why not try something new today!

Reflection

1. Try something new.

2. What new experience have you been putting off out of fear?

3. What is something you learned about yourself from a new experience?

20.Failure

Week 4: Thursday

"Brothers, I do not consider that I have made it my own. But one thing I do: forgetting what lies behind and straining forward to what lies ahead, I press on toward the goal for the prize of the upward call of God in Christ Jesus."
(Philippians 3:13–14, ESV)

Success is born out of failure

I have learned more from failure than I have ever learned from success. Success often leads to complacency. We take things for granted.

Learn to embrace failure. Here is an example. Say you are in sales. For every twenty calls you make, you attain one sale. That means you will fail nineteen times before you close on a single deal. So, what do you do when you make the call and are rejected? Do you wallow in pity that you missed out on a potential sale? Or do you rejoice because you know that you are one call closer to closing a deal?

Success in life is rarely experienced without failure. Success often comes as a result of a series of failures. Failure teaches us humility. It teaches us perseverance. It leads to a greater appreciation when we experience success. Every failure means we are one step closer to breakthrough.

A way to the other side

At some point, you will hit a brick wall. Then, there is a decision to be made. You can give up. Or you can figure out a way to go over or around it. The only way to lose in life is when you give up. And if God is with you, there is always a way to the other side.

In our verse for today, the Apostle Paul talks about "straining forward" to what lies ahead. He presses on toward the goal for the prize of the upward call of God. He acknowledges that it is difficult to keep moving forward, but keep moving forward!

Keep failure in perspective, recognizing failure will ultimately move us forward if we are willing to embrace it. Growth is not linear. For every two steps forward there may be one step back. Sometimes the biggest steps forward come on the heels of the biggest steps backward.

Best of Luck

Every once in a while, someone will wish me good luck. My typical response is "I don't need luck." They look at me a bit curious. I tell them that I have something better than luck. I have God on my side.

I believe that when I live faithful, God will open doors of opportunity. When things don't go the way I hope, I consider it a teaching moment. I ask what is God instilling in me?

What you don't see with most every person who caught that lucky break is the 100 bad breaks they experienced beforehand. But when the opportunity came, they were ready to seize it. We are not victims of fate. We are more than conquerors through Christ. Make your own luck and embrace failure.

Reflection

1. What have you learned from failure?

2. Where is God calling you to embrace failure today and not give up?

3. Do you believe in luck? Why or why not?

21.Fitness

Week 4: Friday

"Or do you not know that your body is a temple of the Holy Spirit within you, whom you have from God? You are not your own..."
(1 Corinthians 6:19, ESV)

The Bible does not discuss the topic of fitness in great detail. One verse that is often associated with the topic is 1 Corinthians 6:19. Here we are told that our bodies are temples of the Holy Spirit. But the context of this verse is not about fitness. It is about sexual immorality.

One of the reasons I believe that fitness is not specifically addressed is because the world of the Bible was different than today. Life was much more physically demanding. Primary occupations were farming, shepherding, and fishing. If you had to travel anywhere, you would walk. People were naturally fit.

Today, our lifestyles are much more sedentary. We sit for long periods of time. We have jobs where we sit at desks behind computer screens. When we travel, we sit in our cars. We come home in the evening, and we sit on our couches watching TV.

Food is also much different today. Food was much more natural and organic. You got it directly from the ground. Today we fill our bodies with processed food. There is a plethora of unhealthy foods that are readily and conveniently available in our local supermarkets. Many of these choices simply were not available when the Bible was written.

Obesity has become an epidemic in America. We have limited levels of energy because of a lack of fitness. Just as we are called to be good stewards of our money, we are also called to be stewards of our bodies which are created after the image of God. Ill health has negative consequences on our ability to serve God, our families, the church, and our communities. It is something to take seriously if we take seriously our calling from God to serve this world

If you are like most Americans, your fitness level is not where it should be. Get active! Instead of sitting down to watch TV, take a walk. Or put on an exercise video. Everyone is always fighting for the closest parking spot. Instead of looking for the closest parking spot, find a spot in the back. I am sure there will be plenty of spots, and you will have an opportunity for a nice walk. Another simple thing you can do is take the stairs instead of the elevator. The point is there are already ample opportunities to be more active if we open our eyes.

Then consider what you eat. Someone shared with me that we often eat food for how it tastes. But what if we started eating food for how it makes us feel. I have a sweet tooth. I love the taste of cookies, candy, and ice cream. What I don't like is the crash after the initial sugar rush. This knowledge helps me avoid junk food and search for healthier alternatives that boost levels of energy and alertness.

Most all of us have things we can do to improve our fitness. You don't need to join the gym to be more active. You don't need to sign up for the latest dieting fad to eat better. Fitness starts with having the right mentality. It is about small choices we make throughout the day. If you want to start some regimented exercise program or sign up for some super diet, go for it. But it will go further to reconsider many of the individual choices you make throughout the day.

Reflection

1. Do you see fitness as a spiritual matter?

2. What are some simple ways you can be more active while doing the things you already do?

3. What is your motivation for eating? How might you shift that motivation?

22. Vision

Week 4: Saturday

"Having the eyes of your hearts enlightened, that you may know what is the hope to which he has called you, what are the riches of his glorious inheritance in the saints, and what is the immeasurable greatness of his power toward us who believe, according to the working of his great might . . ." (Ephesians 1:18–19, ESV)

Where are you going?

Our family has been talking about summer vacation. We have been considering different destinations. It is fun to think about all the different possibilities of the place we could go. We could go to the beach, the mountains, or the city. The possibilities are endless.

But at some point, we need to decide where we are going. We have to pick one destination for our vacation. Once we know where we are going, we can start making our plans. We will get travel information to find some of the fun things to do in the place we are visiting. We will make a packing list of all the things we will need to bring with us. We will also determine the best way to get there. Will we fly, or will we drive? If we drive, what route will we take?

The basic principle here is that the destination will determine the plan. We will figure out where we are going, and then figure out how to get there. This is how life works. Start with the end in mind. If you never determine the destination, you will never get there.

Many of us don't know where we are going. We don't have a vision for our life. We wake up each morning hoping to just get through the day. Then we get up the next day and repeat the same thing. We are left to survive rather than thrive. That changes when we have a vision where we are going.

See the Big Picture

As a Pastor, I officiate many funerals. One of the things I share in most funeral messages is that one day we will be the one whose family and friends are gathered to remember our life. The question is what will they say about us when that day comes? What is the legacy that we will leave?

Death is not something we may think about. It is something we may try to avoid thinking about at all costs. But it is a reality that we cannot get past. There is nothing more certain in life. So as much as we might try to avoid it, whether we like it or not, we will be made to face it.

Funerals may seem like morbid events, but as believers, we have a different mindset. God did not create us for this earth. We are just passing through. Heaven is our home. And we will dwell in eternity much longer than we will dwell in this place. To have a vision of this reality changes everything.

There is a picture of a sculpture I will sometimes share in my funeral messages. It is called "Come Unto Me" by Jerry Anderson. The sculpture has an old lady who is entering a doorway. The door represents death. She is hunched over. She is holding a cane in her hands. You can almost feel her pain as you look at her face. She is looking away from the door. She is looking backward. She is looking to the past. There may be regrets that she is pondering. There may be guilt. It is difficult to look at her.

But when she passes through the door, everything changes. On the other side of the doorway is another woman who has been made new. The wrinkles, the pain, and the regret are all gone. She is no longer looking back. She is looking ahead. And where is she looking? She is looking to Jesus. She is no longer limping with a cane but running to embrace her Savior.

Vision changes everything. As we seek vision, there is no greater vision than Jesus. Imagine how different the statue would be if the elderly lady had the vision of Jesus before she died. The same is true for you.

I leave you today with the lyrics of the beloved hymn, Be Thou My Vision:

> *Be Thou my Vision, O Lord of my heart*
> *Naught be all else to me, save that Thou art*
> *Thou my best Thought, by day or by night*
> *Waking or sleeping, Thy presence my light*

Be Thou my Wisdom, and Thou my true Word
I ever with Thee and Thou with me, Lord
Thou my great Father, I Thy true son
Thou in me dwelling, and I with Thee one

Reflection

1. Are you living to survive the day, or do you have a greater vision?

2. How does death empower you to live and embrace the present?

3. How does the vision of Jesus change your life?

Week 5

Theme for the Week: Relationships

"The glory that you have given me I have given to them, that they may be one even as we are one..."
(John 17:22, ESV)

This week we will be exploring relationships. You may be familiar with Maslov's Hierarchy of Needs. The List includes:

1. Physiological needs
2. Safety needs
3. Love and belonging
4. Esteem
5. Self-actualization
6. Self-transcendence

The first two things on that list are a matter of life and death. They are of first importance. But you will notice that the third thing on the list is "love and belonging." It would be easy to dismiss this need as a matter of life and death, but if we understand the true importance of this need, we will recognize it is also a matter of life and death. Consider this statement from the US Surgeon General:

"The greatest public health crisis in America is not cancer or heart disease. It's social isolation. Loneliness." – Dr. Vivek Murthy, the Surgeon General of the United States

Isolation from others will lead to a whole host of problems:

"Social isolation is as potent a cause of early death as smoking 15 cigarettes a day; loneliness, research suggests, is twice as deadly as obesity. Dementia, high blood pressure, alcoholism and accidents – all these, like depression, paranoia, anxiety and suicide, become more prevalent when connections are cut. We cannot cope alone." – George Monbiot (Journalist)

Maybe you saw the movie Castaway. Tom Hanks plays, Chuck Noland, a FedEx employee who is stranded on a deserted island after a plane crash. Without anyone around, he finds companionship in a volleyball he names Wilson. The extreme isolation leads him to put his life at risk on the open sea for the slim chance he might find civilization.

When we see a person who commits a violent crime, we will often find out that the person was isolated from others. The people interviewed on the news will describe him as a social outcast, living on the fringe, and who kept to himself. In other words, he was a loner! Love and belonging are more important than we realize. This is because:

God created us as relational beings

When God created humankind, this is what he said:

> *Then the LORD God said, "It is* **not good that the man should be alone**; *I will make him a helper fit for him." (Genesis 2:18, ESV)*

Notice he said that it is not good that man should be alone. It is part of creating humankind in his image because God himself exists in relationship.

> *Then God said, "***Let us*** make man in our image, after our likeness." (Genesis 1:26, ESV)*

There is the Trinity Godhead. God is one God in three persons. There is Father, Son, and Holy Spirit. The Hebrew word for God is Elohim. The construction of the word itself is plural. There is plurality in this single God. As God himself lives relationally, he creates us to live relationally.

When Jesus came to this earth, he ministered to thousands of people. But he still kept close at hand 12 close companions to do life together. God wired us for connection. And when we are disconnected, we will short-circuit. There are great dangers when we don't live as God created us to live.

With all this in mind, we will turn our attention this week to discovering deeper and more intimate relationships.

- **Monday:** People
- **Tuesday:** Grace

- **Wednesday:** Forgiveness
- **Thursday:** Adventure
- **Friday:** Respect
- **Saturday:** Accountability

23.People

Week 5: Monday

"For what will it profit a man if he gains the whole world and forfeits his soul? Or what shall a man give in return for his soul?"
(Matthew 16:26, ESV)

Promises in the Plural

Many of the promises in the Bible are written in the plural. Because we live in a culture that values individualism, we miss that many of the promises are not given to "me" alone, but "us" together. In our English language, the word "you" can be plural or singular. "You" can be a group of people or it can be one person. It is not the same with the Biblical languages. "You" is designated as either singular or plural. So, when we read the Bible in these original languages, it is clear whether it is a community or individual that is being addressed. We don't get the same benefit with our English translation.

Consider the verses on the next page where I have added "all" to designate the plural "you." Consider how it changes the way we read these texts:

"But **(you all)** *seek first the kingdom of God and his righteousness, and all these things will be added to you* **(all)**.*" (Matthew 6:33, ESV)*

"For I know the plans I have for you **(all)**, *declares the LORD, plans for welfare and not for evil, to give you* **(all)** *a future and a hope."* *(Jeremiah 29:11, ESV)*

"(You all) *go therefore and make disciples of all nations."* *(Matthew 28:19, ESV)*

Maybe the reason that we don't see the promises of God fulfilled in a greater measure is that we have been going at it alone.

Are you going it alone?

More than half of Americans admit they have no one with whom they can talk about their personal troubles or successes outside of their closest family members. We are living in increasing isolation, and it is not good for us. Where do you fit into this picture?

Do you have a close and personal friend? Do you have someone that you can talk about stresses and anxieties in your life?

The men reading this are more likely to say "no" to this question. Men tend to be more isolated. Most American men have no friends. They have acquaintances and interact with people all day long. But they rarely have true friends. With increased workloads and business, we often find ourselves spread thin and don't make the commitment and time for friendships. I wonder if this is one of the reasons men tend to die sooner than women.

Be a friend

One of the most popular descriptions people have of their church is that their church is a "friendly church." But it doesn't mean much to be friendly. The checkout lady at the supermarket is friendly. But I don't go to the supermarket to meet the friendly lady at the checkout. People don't care if you have a "friendly church." What they care about is if we will be their friend. What they wonder about is if they can find connection and community.

We have a lot of chit-chat in our churches. We talk about the sports team, the weather, or the headlines in the news. And there is nothing wrong with talking about these things. But it is important to go beyond these things.

I need people to ask me the hard questions. I need people who are going to make me a better pastor, a better husband, a better Christian, a better father. The Bible tells us iron sharpens iron (see Proverbs 27:17). We need to be that iron for each other. That does not happen by accident. It takes intentionality. It takes discipline. It takes valuing people and the importance of relationships.

One thing I have learned over the years is that to make a friend you need to be a friend. When you genuinely care for other people, they will tend to care for you. The more you give, the more you get. You will reap what you sow. So, start sowing the seeds of friendship. Make a friend! Be a friend!

Reflection

1. Why are relationships important? What are the consequences of isolation?

2. Do you have a close friend in whom you can confide?

3. How can you be a friend today?

24.Grace

Week 5: Tuesday

"Put on then, as God's chosen ones, holy and beloved, compassionate hearts, kindness, humility, meekness, and patience, bearing with one another and, if one has a complaint against another, forgiving each other; as the Lord has forgiven you, so you also must forgive."
(Colossians 3:12 – 13, ESV)

One thing I have learned is I'm not perfect. I've made my share of mistakes. I need grace. I need others to be patient and understanding with me. We are all like that. We could all use a little more grace extended our way.

As I recognize my need for grace, I understand that others need grace as well. Be patient with others and give them the benefit of the doubt. As the Scripture tells us, be slow to take offense (see James 1:19-20).

But we are often quick to take offense. I sometimes wonder if we go out of our way to look for ways to be offended by the words and actions of others. When it comes to being offended, there are two types of people who offend us. There are those who don't intend and those who do intend to offend us.

Unintentional Offense

In Colossians, the Apostle Paul tells us with compassion, kindness, humility, meekness, and patience to bear with one another. It's easy to get upset and angry with people for their shortcomings, even when they never intend to give offense.

I know there are many times in my life where the message received by another person, was not the message I intended. This is especially true in electronic communications such as email. A general rule I follow is to never be offended by something someone shares in an email. There is too much room for misinterpretation when the person is not face-to-face with you.

Even when you are with a person face-to-face, be patient. Before you get offended, make sure that you seek to understand. Consider if you have truly received the message they intended to share with you.

Intentional Offense

While I believe that we are often more guilty of taking offense than we at giving offense, there are plenty of times when people do indeed intend to offend us.

One thing that has helped me to be more patient and grace-filled with people is to recognize that many of them do not have Jesus in their life. They are missing out on the peace, joy, and hope that he has to offer. Their lives are filled with sorrow and frustration. They are not living with any higher purpose other than to make it through the day.

Hurting people hurt other people. The hurt that they are attempting to pile on to you is often a cry for help. They just don't know how to ask for help.

They need grace, not your offense. Offer words of kindness or an act of grace. They need it in a big way! It may be something as simple as offering a smile or a compliment. Maybe you have heard it said, "kill them with kindness." It's not the other person to kill, but the hurt inside them.

> *"A soft answer turns away wrath, but a harsh word stirs up anger." (Proverbs 15:1, ESV)*

Walk Away

Finally, sometimes it is better just to walk away. There are times when love and kindness will only be met with resistance. A person's heart may be so hardened that they will refuse any help that is given. I am reminded of Jesus' words:

> *"And wherever they do not receive you, when you leave that town shake off the dust from your feet as a testimony against them." (Luke 9:5, ESV)*

You can pray for the person. You can feel sorrow for the other person. But sometimes it is best just to let go of the offense and to move on.

Reflection

1. Is there a time when others were offended by something you said when you never intended to give offense?

2. How can you better seek understanding before taking offense?

3. How do you know when it is time to walk away from a situation or person?

25.Forgiveness

Week 5: Wednesday

"Be kind to one another, tenderhearted, forgiving one another, as God in Christ forgave you."
(Ephesians 4:32, ESV)

The Cost of Forgiveness

Forgiveness does not come easy. Jesus died for our forgiveness. There was a price paid. When we go back to the Old Testament, a sacrifice was offered for sin. You would take an innocent lamb. The lamb had not done anything, but your sin would cost that lamb his life.

When you entered into the temple, you would sense death. You would hear the lambs being slaughtered. You would smell the flesh being burned. You would see the blood draining off the altar. It was rather grotesque. It was a powerful visual reminder of the consequence of sin.

It is different for us today. The religious ritual of forgiveness is much cleaner. We confess our sins in the presence of God. The pastor announces words of absolution. You might make the sign of the cross from your head to your heart and shoulder to shoulder. There is no fire or blood.

Then, we approach the altar. We receive in the bread and wine, the very body and blood of Jesus. But it does not look like flesh or blood. It looks like bread and wine. It tastes like bread and wine. When we receive these, the pastor says, "take eat and take drink for the forgiveness of your sins." Again, everything is neat and clean!

But remember what is behind these acts. It is the sacrifice of Jesus. He was the Lamb of God who takes away the sin of the world. His sacrifice on the cross was hideous. If you ever watched the movie the Passion of Christ, you start to get a sense of the horror. Lutheran pastor and theologian, Dietrich Bonhoeffer said, "Grace is free, but it is not cheap." Indeed, the free gift of forgiveness came at a tremendous cost. The cost was the innocent, bitter suffering and death of Jesus.

We Forgive as God has Forgiven Us

When we read Ephesians 4:32, we read that we are to forgive one another. It is not easy to forgive. There is sacrifice involved. Anyone who says forgiveness is easy has never truly forgiven. It is easier to hold on to bitterness and grudges than it is to forgive. But it is through forgiveness that we experience freedom. It is freedom from sin and freedom to experience fulfillment in our relationships.

Forgiveness is critical for relationships. I am a sinner, and you are a sinner. We have that in common. If we spend enough time with each other, there will come a time when I will sin against you, and you will sin against me. We are human. It is part of our nature, and there is no getting around that. If we are going stay in relationship, we must learn to forgive one another. Otherwise, there will be a wedge that is driven between us. A divide will hinder true intimacy. We will go our separate ways and move on from one superficial relationship to another.

Forgiveness is a bridge. It is sin that divides, but forgiveness that unites. The forgiveness that Jesus won on the cross was so that we could live in relationship with God. It was so that we could know God. It was so we could approach his throne of grace in prayer. It was so that we could stand before him in eternity.

The forgiveness of Jesus also empowers our forgiveness. We see we have been forgiven a tremendous debt. How insignificant become the things we are unwilling to forgive. Our sacrifice to forgive may be difficult, but our sacrifice pales in comparison to the great sacrifice Jesus made to forgive us.

Reflection
1. Why is forgiveness so difficult?

2. Is there anyone you need to reach out to and forgive?

3. Is there anyone you need to ask for forgiveness?

26.Adventure

Week 5: Thursday

"Yet it was kind of you to share my trouble."
(Philippians 4:14, ESV)

Today's devotion is more directed to the men reading this than the women. Women tend to have more true friendships than men do. I see this in church. On any given Sunday, there are typically more women in church than men. This is true in almost any church in America. The women come, and they interact with one another. They talk about life and all the other things that women talk about.

But for many of these women, their husbands are sitting at home, alone. Many of these men are not interested in the potentially awkward social interactions of a Sunday morning. They isolate themselves from others.

Beyond the church setting, there are many men in America who do not have any friends. They tend to be loners. They may interact with people all day long at work, but at the end of the day they come home and have no one to talk with about the important things in life. If their marriage is struggling or they have problems at work, they will internalize it all.

There is a difference between the way men and women typically interact. When you observe women interacting, they will typically do so face-to-face. But when men interact, they will do so shoulder-to-shoulder. Men will bond through sharing a common purpose and moving together in the same direction for greater things. It is not "connection" that men seek as much as it is belonging to something bigger than themselves.

You think about the bond of men who have gone to war together. They are a band of brothers. Think about men on the athletic field in competition. These men are striving together for a common purpose that creates an alliance. These are the men in life that we, as men, are drawn towards.

As men, we are looking to go somewhere, fix something, or fight someone. We want to be part of and share in doing something great. This is a big reason we often see more women in church than men. In church, we talk about love and connection with God in our worship. We sing songs about how much we love Jesus. That is good, but as men, we want to do something. We want to make something happen.

Don't miss out on the warrior Jesus, who was a kingdom of darkness conqueror, and who invites us to join him on the adventure. The invitation is to join with him for a wild ride, living a purpose that is bigger than anyone of us. The life of faith is not about sitting in a pew, but living as more than a conqueror through Jesus

Christ. It is fighting for all that is good and right. So, let's live the adventure together.

Reflection

1. Why do you think there are more women in church than men?

2. What are the differences between the way men bond and women bond?

3. How can you join Jesus in an adventure of a lifetime and partner with others to live a purpose bigger than yourself for God's kingdom?

27.Respect

Week 5: Friday

"Submitting to one another out of reverence for Christ." (Ephesians 5:21, ESV)

R–E–S–P–E–C–T. All Aretha Franklin asked for was a little respect. And it is something God tells us to offer to one another. Ephesians 5 says to respect one another out of reverence for Christ. You cannot have a successful marriage or any other relationship without a healthy dose of respect. Respect is what makes relationships tick.

What does it mean to respect? To me, it means to treat someone with honor. It is to hold others in admiration. It means to treat them, at minimum, as an equal. If you have employees who work under you, value them for their service and the contribution they are making to your business. You could not do what you do without them. Value them as more than labor, but as human beings.

Maybe you have read some online forums that turn ugly. Instead of trading opinions, the forum becomes about trading insults. It is no longer about debating ideas but debating character. It is a microcosm of what is happening in our country. It's okay to disagree. It is another matter to disrespect someone as a person.

A few years ago, I was pulled over for speeding. I don't think I was actually speeding. I was angry. I was upset. I must say I was not as respectful as I could have been to the officer. I drove away from that encounter with a ticket in hand.

A few years later, I slowed down at a stop sign. I saw another car was coming and was a bit impatient. I knew that if I stopped, I would have to wait for the car to go by. I just rolled up to the stop sign, and then punched it. However, the car that was approaching was a police car. I was caught. But this time, my interaction with the officer was very different. I offered the respect and courtesy. This time I walked away with a warning.

I don't know if my interactions with the officers made the difference in getting a ticket versus getting a warning. I would like to think that they did. I cannot guarantee that offering respect to a police officer will get you away with just a warning. But there is a saying: you catch more flies with honey than vinegar.

In general, people are more inclined to help you and will go out of their way for you when you treat them with respect. It will not happen all the time. But it will happen more often than not.

When we don't get our way, our inclination is to complain louder. But complaining louder rarely gets us anywhere. We can express our displeasure and let people know we are disappointed. But do it with courtesy and respect.

Reflection

1. What does respect mean to you?

2. Is there anyone in your life you have not been giving the respect that Christ has called you to give respect?

3. How has offering respect gotten you farther than offering disrespect?

28.Accountability

Week 5: Saturday

"So then each of us will give an account of himself to God." (Romans 14:12, ESV)

How are you doing with those New Year's resolutions? If you are like most people, you forgot about them long ago. The eagerness you had when you showed up at the gym on January 1 is long gone.

Why do we struggle with these commitments we make? There may be a good number of reasons, but I believe the biggest reason is that we have no accountability. If you are serious about commitment, build in accountability. If you are serious about showing up at the gym, get a personal trainer who will work with you. If you can't afford a trainer, then get a buddy to come with you.

When you show up at work on Monday morning, it is because you have accountability. The boss at work holds you accountable to be there. If you do not show up, you will be reprimanded and eventually fired. Work is a commitment you keep because you know there are consequences if you don't.

The difference with New Year's resolutions is that we make the commitment to ourselves alone. There is no one holding us accountable. We have no one to answer to but ourselves. If we don't follow through with our commitment, the only person we are letting down is ourselves.

There is a reason a group like AA assigns you a sponsor. If you are to make the commitment to give up alcohol and conquer the addiction, you need help. When you know that you have someone else to answer to, you are more likely to follow through because you don't want to let them down. We have an easier time disappointing ourselves than we do disappointing other people. A friend of mine says that "you cannot self–help your way to God."

You Are Already Accountable

At the end of our life, we will all stand before God in judgment. In Romans 14:12, it says that we will all give an account of ourselves. We will answer for all the things we did or did not do with our life on this earth. If you are a believer, you can be sure that all these things will be forgiven but recognize that not all will be rewarded.

The point is that you are already accountable. You may not recognize the accountability that exists in your life. But as you recognize your eternal accountability, it will give you an incentive for building temporal accountability.

Do More

Do you want more in life? Do you want to pursue greater things in life? Stop telling yourself what you want in life and start telling other people. It may be a scary thing because it means you will need to start doing what you say you are going to do. Most of us resist accountability. Many people fear accountability. Accountability makes us vulnerable. It raises the bar of expectation. But it also opens the door for us to walk in greater abundance and experience greater fulfillment.

"And though a man might prevail against one who is alone, two will withstand him—a threefold cord is not quickly broken."
(Ecclesiastes 4:12, ESV)

Reflection

1. Do you have people in your life who hold you accountable?

2. Why do you resist accountability?

3. Make a list of 3 people who might serve as accountability partners. Different areas of our life may require different accountability partners.

Week 6

Theme for the Week: Serving

"But whoever would be great among you must be your servant, and whoever would be first among you must be your slave, even as the Son of Man came not to be served but to serve, and to give his life as a ransom for many."
(Matthew 20:26b–28, ESV)

What is the greatest privilege in life? Living in luxury? Having servants who will come at your beck and call? This is what convention will tell us. Privilege is being wealthy beyond our wildest dreams so that we never need to lift a finger. We think of the lifestyles of the rich and famous as privilege.

But true fulfillment is not found in solely living. It is found in giving. True fulfillment does not come by breathing and taking up space. True fulfillment is discovered through what we do with this life. Being served and waited on by others is nice, but if that is all our life involves, it will lead to emptiness.

What does Jesus say? He says that whoever would be great (whoever wants a great life) must become a servant. Jesus himself did not come to be served, but to serve.

We were created to serve. Most importantly, we were created to serve the living God. God created you to make a difference. God created you to change the world and to make it a better place, one person at a time.

Our theme this week this is serving. The six things we will look at are:

- **Monday:** Compassion
- **Tuesday:** Prayer
- **Wednesday:** Generosity
- **Thursday:** Purpose
- **Friday:** Compliments
- **Saturday:** Gifts & Abilities

29. Compassion

Week 6: Monday

"Blessed be the God and Father of our Lord Jesus Christ, the Father of mercies and God of all comfort, who comforts us in all our affliction, so that we may be able to comfort those who are in any affliction, with the comfort with which we ourselves are comforted by God."
(2 Corinthians 1:3–4, ESV)

When we look at the world around us, we will see there is so much pain, hurt, and sorrow. The need is great. I could rehearse a bunch of statistics, but you don't need statistics. Every day people die of hunger. They suffer from illness caused by unsanitary drinking water. Slavery did not end with the Civil War, and is very much a reality today. The illnesses that you and I go to a doctor to have treated are a death sentence in many countries. The list goes on.

The sad thing is that it does not need to be this way. There are more than enough resources to go around to end much of this suffering. Often, the problem is not a lack of resources; it is a lack of compassion. We are so self-absorbed in our 1st world problems, we don't give much thought to these other problems.

Does what break God's heart, break your heart? We may wonder why God does not do something about the great suffering in this world. The answer is that he already has done something. He created you. He gave you gifts, talents, and abilities. He put resources at your disposal. What do we think it means when Jesus says to seek first the kingdom of God? His reign is ushered in when we offer compassion.

You may not be able to end world hunger. But you can end hunger for some. If you have compassion, you can make a difference. If more of us responded with compassion rather than apathy, the world would be a much different place.

A phrase I heard a few years back was "live simply so that others can simply live." But we often get self-absorbed in maintaining our lifestyles and keeping up with the Joneses. The biggest help we give is helping ourselves. How will we answer God about what we did with all that he gave to us?

Get Involved

I am excited to have been part of an effort to feed the hungry. Last year, our church partnered with an organization called Numana (numanainc.com) to package more than 80,000 meals for children in Haiti. The meals went to Mission of Hope, Haiti (mohhaiti.org) who feeds 93,000 children every day. There are still 70,000 children on their waiting list. The meals we packed helped take some of the 70,000 children off the waiting list.

This is an event we are organizing again this year. It was not easy to accomplish last year, but it was so worth it. We need to do this again. It was through this that we experienced a Kingdom victory.

In the end, I want to encourage you to do something! It does not need to be an effort to feed the hungry. There are so many other needs. You don't need to look hard. Have the heart, and God will show you the way. Thank you in advance for your compassion.

Reflection

1. What is a need in this world that you can identify?

2. How does it make you feel when you serve the needs of others? Why do you think it feels so good?

3. Do something!

30.Prayer

Week 6: Tuesday

*"First of all, then, I urge that supplications,
prayers, intercessions, and thanksgivings be made
for all people, for kings and all who are in high
positions, that we may lead a peaceful and quiet
life, godly and dignified in every way."*
(1 Timothy 2:1−2, ESV)

It might seem obvious that prayer is not something to
give up for Lent. Lent is a season to focus on the
spiritual disciplines. But as we think about the theme of
serving this week, we consider a specific focus of
prayer. It is about offering prayer as intercession on
behalf of others.

Paul tells young Timothy to pray for all people. This
includes offering prayer on our behalf, but also on
behalf of others. Sometimes we may tell people that we
can at least pray for them. But that statement is wrong.
Prayer is not the least we can do for someone. It is the
most we can do for someone.

Martin Luther would say that when he got especially
busy, he would devote the 3 or 4 most productive hours

of his day to prayer. It says much about his belief in the power of prayer. God can do more in those 3 or 4 hours than we could ever do.

Something happens in us when we intentionally pray for others. Our perspective on the world changes. The way we look at other people is different. The people you were once angry towards, you now feel compassion. It might even happen that as you begin to pray that God will move you to action. He will start give you a heart of compassion in an area you once held apathy.

Many of us are not good at carving time out for prayer. When we do make time for prayer, our prayers are often focused on ourselves. But there are so many people for whom we can pray. Consider the list of 40 people for whom you could pray:

1. Your spouse

2. Your children

3. Your parents

4. Your friends

5. Brothers and sisters in Christ at your local church

6. Your pastor and his family

7. People who serve and protect you (first responders and military)

8. Those who govern (local, state, and national)

9. Your enemies and those who would do you harm

10.   Those who have offended you

11.   The hungry

12. The homeless

13. Those in prison

14. Educators

15. Missionaries serving in foreign countries

16. Those experiencing divorce (especially children)

17. Medical workers

18. The addicted

19. The lonely and depressed

20. Those who have suffered the loss of a loved one and live in grief

21. Those facing cancer or illness

22. Those who are living as refugees from war or persecution

23. The persecuted church

24. The sex-trafficked

25. Victims of racial discrimination and violence

26. Those who suffer from domestic abuse

27. Those facing their last days on earth

28. The next generation and challenges/temptations they face

29. Entrepreneurs and Small Business owners

30. Creatives, artists, and designers who make the world a more beautiful place

31. Volunteers who serve the need of others with the expectation of nothing in return.

32. Those who have wandered from the faith or have a lukewarm faith.

33. People who live apart from the grace of God, and have not received the gift of salvation through Jesus Christ.

34.

35.

36.

37.

38.

39.

40.

I did not complete the list. I left the last seven blank. There are certainly other people and situations for whom we can pray. Take some time to fill in the blanks and pray for these people.

Reflection

1. Pray for others

2. Add additional groups of people for whom we can pray.

3. Share your prayer request with me at philressler.com/prayer.

31.Generosity

Week 6: Wednesday

*"The point is this: whoever sows sparingly will
also reap sparingly, and whoever sows bountifully
will also reap bountifully."*
(2 Corinthians 9:6, ESV)

2 Corinthians 9:6 is one of the most powerful passages
of Scripture. It is common sense, but it is not common
practice. Many of us sow sparingly but hope to reap
abundantly.

There is often a correlation between debt and
generosity. I don't have any verification of this as fact,
but see it more as a general observation. Those who are
most in debt are often the least generous. On the one
hand, there is an excuse not to be generous because of
the debt. But even more important is the mindset that
leads to debt.

Debt is caused by a spirit of poverty. There is a
perception of scarcity. It is the idea that I need to hold
on to what I have and not let it go. I will hoard what I
have in fear that I will be left in want. This spirit makes
me especially susceptible to be manipulated into

thinking I need things I can't afford to make me content, happy, and fulfilled.

The spirit of poverty has its grip on many of us. It's got its grip on many churches and ministries. Our effectiveness is thwarted by worrying about "paying the bills."

The antidote to perceived scarcity is to practice generosity. We cannot out-give God. A more abundant harvest comes as a result of planting more seed. The more seed that is planted this year will result in the ability to plant even more seed in the following year. Instead of living with perceived scarcity, recognize the abundance of God. Recognize that he is the provider. Recognize that the one who gave you everything can give you even more.

In the Parable of the Talents (see Luke 19:11-27), the first two servants put to work what the master had given them. God prospers their work and the result is that they were entrusted with more. God rewards faithfulness. The third servant hoarded what he had. But in the end, even what little he had was taken away. It was not about what they had. It was about what they did with what they had.

Eliminating debt starts with eliminating the mindset that causes debt. Live faithfully with what you have been given, and trust in God's supply. Loosen your grip on stuff to allow yourself to take hold of God's blessings.

Reflection

1. Do you agree or disagree that debt and lack of generosity are related?

2. How has a lack of generosity been detrimental in your life?

3. How can you specifically practice generosity with your time, treasure, and talent?

32.Purpose

Week 6: Thursday

"For we are his workmanship, created in Christ Jesus for good works, which God prepared beforehand, that we should walk in them."
(Ephesians 2:10, ESV)

Make you purpose

Some people will talk about finding their purpose. They talk about it as if it is something that is missing. It might be buried under a rock. Or it might be hidden in a closet. They feel they need to look in the right place to discover it. When they finally find it, they will be able to do what they were made to do.

But if you are looking for your purpose, you will be looking your whole life. Purpose is not something to be found. It is not something that is hidden. It is something to which to take hold. You don't find your purpose. You create your purpose. You have already been given it. It is before you.

That is a different mindset. You are not a victim of fate. There is not some mystical destiny that you happen upon. God has empowered you through his Holy Spirit to do immeasurably more than you imagine. God will take you places you never dreamed. But it starts with doing something today. It is taking hold of what is before you. It's following him! Stop waiting and start doing. There are things that you have the ability to do, but you don't even realize that you have the ability because you have never tried.

When Jesus called his disciples, he said: "Follow me, and I will make you fishers of men." (Matthew 4:19, ESV) The text says they immediately left their nets and followed him. They were fishermen of fish. What did they know about fishing men? But when Jesus gave the invitation, they didn't question it. They went.

There is a saying that God does not call the qualified, but he qualifies the called. Here is what I know. There are opportunities before you right now that God has given you to serve your purpose. I also know that you probably feel unqualified to step up to these things. This is where faith comes into play. You trust that God will equip you. You trust he will give you the strength, the knowledge, the people, and the resources to make it happen.

A God Thing

I shared with you three days ago about how our church served the hungry. The original effort was to prepare 20,000 meals for children of Haiti.

After returning from a Haiti Mission Trip, I felt led to host this event. We shared the vision for this event and what it would take in terms of money and people to make it happen.

After only two weeks of fundraising, God supplied everything we needed. We celebrated the accomplishment of this goal, and even had our church choir singing the Hallelujah Chorus during Lent. We never expected us to cross the fundraising threshold so fast. But God has a way of showing up.

With more than a month left before the event, it would have been easy to have doubled the goal. That would have been comfortable. But we believed that God would have us go beyond what was comfortable. So, we quadrupled the goal, and God made it happen. Our tiny church, with the help of many others, did a great thing.

I believe God led us to this place, and it was his will to have made it happen. We trusted him to make it happen, rather than relying on our ability.

Your purpose will change

Finally, know that what gets you up in the morning will change. Before I was married and before I had children, my purpose was different. Marriage and children changed my life purpose. My priorities shifted from career to marriage and family. One day, my children will leave our home. I will still be their father, but I will play a different role in their lives. My purpose will change. The point is not to think that you have one ultimate thing to do in your life. Every day, we all serve multiple purposes. Every day, there are multiple opportunities. It's time to go. Let's do it.

Reflection

1. List some purposes God has given you.

2. How do you recognize when God is calling you to serve?

3. Where is God stretching you beyond what is comfortable?

33.Compliments

Week 6: Friday

"Let the word of Christ dwell in you richly, teaching and admonishing one another in all wisdom, singing psalms and hymns and spiritual songs, with thankfulness in your hearts to God."
(Colossians 3:16, ESV)

I hate receiving compliments said no one ever. We all appreciate words of affirmation. There is not one person without doubts and insecurities. If you peel enough layers of the onion back, you will discover that the most confident people are not as confident as they appear.

We live in a critical world. There is more than enough criticism to go around. It is a way of life to criticize politicians in the Capital, supervisors at work, pastors in the church, and spouses at home. Ask yourself if you have a complimentary or critical spirit? Are you more likely to compliment or complain?

There are enough people tearing down others. We need more people to build up others and be encouragers for Christ. This is especially true in the church. Colossians

3:16 tells us to let the Word of Christ dwell in us to teach and admonish one another. If it is the Word of God that is dwelling in us, it is with grace that we will lead.

Certainly, there is a time to confront. But the opportunity to confront is born out of a building a healthy and positive relationship. You earn the right to confront and criticize.

To Compliment is Not to Flatter

There is a difference between being complimentary towards someone and practicing flattery. To compliment another is to build them up for the sake of building them up. Flattery is about manipulating another person to get what you want. There is a fine line. Make sure your words of affirmation are from the heart.

Avoid Sarcasm

We use sarcasm in fun and playful ways. But sarcasm is more dangerous than most of us realize. It is like playing with fire. We may say something in good humor, but the sarcasm can easily be missed. That message sent in a playful way is easily received with all seriousness. The humor is missed, and the person on the other end is wounded.

Publicly Compliment

How do you speak about your spouse in public? Are you complimentary towards them? It is one thing to affirm others in private, but it can be especially rewarding when you publicly affirm others. And this is not just for your spouse. It is with other people as well.

Gossip runs rapid. The best way to end a negative conversation about another person is to be complimentary towards that person. Nothing shuts down gossip quicker. A good rule is never say something in a person's absence that you would not say in their presence.

Sometimes It is Better to Say Nothing

There are times when it may be difficult to find anything positive to say. You may feel disappointed by another person. You may feel like lashing out at them. But sometimes it is better to say nothing at all and bite your lip. Instead of being critical – wait, listen, and seek to understand. There may be more to the story than you realize. When we disagree with the choices people make, we may not fully realize the difficulty they had in making the decision. Be careful to criticize people when you don't know the options they had to choose.

Reflection

1. How does it make you feel to be affirmed? How does it make you feel to affirm others?

2. Who do you need to affirm today?

3. How has criticism wounded you? Where do you seek affirmation when you are criticized?

34.Gifts & Abilities

Week 6: Saturday

"And he gave the apostles, the prophets, the evangelists, the shepherds and teachers, to equip the saints for the work of ministry, for building up the body of Christ, until we all attain to the unity of the faith and of the knowledge of the Son of God, to mature manhood, to the measure of the stature of the fullness of Christ, so that we may no longer be children, tossed to and fro by the waves and carried about by every wind of doctrine, by human cunning, by craftiness in deceitful schemes." (Ephesians 4:11–14, ESV)

There are two things I added to the 40 Things NOT to Give Up for Lent list today. They are gifts and abilities! These are all part of a larger category of all the ways in which God equips us to serve. Maybe you have learned about discovering your S.H.A.P.E. These letters stand for:

- **S** - spiritual gifts
- **H** - heart
- **A** - abilities

– **P** - personality

– **E** - experiences

Spiritual gifts are ways in which God supernaturally empowers us for service. These are qualities and characteristics with which we are endowed. They are not learned or acquired. They are given to us by our good and gracious Father in heaven.

Heart is our passion. This is what we get excited about. This is what gets us out of bed before the alarm clock goes off. We have greater motivation in our areas of passion.

Abilities are those things which we have acquired over time. You may have gone to school to learn a skill such as accounting or engineering. You may have studied music or art. Abilities are skills that have come through practice and study.

Personality is about the way you interact with others. Some of us are more introverted, and others of us are more extroverted. Some of us will jump before we look, and others of us will look before we jump.

Experiences are about things we have been through. It is the things you have seen. It is the people with whom you have shared life together. It is the challenges you have overcome.

All these things make you uniquely you. There is no one who has lived with the unique combination of spiritual gifts, heart, abilities, personality, and experiences that you have had. There is no one who will come after you who is like you. You are God's masterpiece. He did not create you to be anyone else. He created you to be who you are and do what you do. Take some time to reflect on what God has given you:

- – What are your spiritual gifts? Have you taken a spiritual gifts inventory?

- – What are your passions? How can these passions be used to bless others?

- – What skills have you acquired? Do you have an outlet to use these skills in a kingdom building manner?

- – Describe your personality. Are you serving in a way that aligns with your personality, or is there a better way to align your serving?

- – How have your life experiences given you the ability to minster compassion to others?

The next step is to put your S.H.A.P.E. to work. Where is God leading you to put those things to work? How can you use these gifts and abilities for God's kingdom?

Reflection

1. Describe your S.H.A.P.E.

2. How can you put these things to work to serve God's kingdom in a unique way?

3. How is knowing your S.H.A.P.E. empowering?

Holy Week

Theme for the Week: Commitment

"I appeal to you therefore, brothers, by the mercies of God, to present your bodies as a living sacrifice, holy and acceptable to God, which is your spiritual worship." (Romans 12:1, ESV)

We have come to the final week of Lent known as Holy Week. It is the week we remember the final days before Jesus would be crucified on the cross. You may be reading this on Palm Sunday which commemorates Jesus' triumphal entry into Jerusalem and points to the coming victory over sin and death.

One of the verses that often stand out for me on Palm Sunday is Luke 9:51. Here is says:

"When the days drew near for him to be taken up, he set his face to go to Jerusalem."
(Luke 9:51, ESV)

The idea that Jesus set his face to Jerusalem implies that he did not look back or look to the side. He resolutely focused on the mission for which he was sent into this world. Nothing was going to stop him. Nothing was going to hold him back. He was going to follow through. He had a commitment to fulfill the will of his Father.

As we are invited to follow Jesus, we are invited to commitment. Life is filled with commitments. There are healthy commitments and unhealthy commitments. There are commitments that are worthy and other commitments that are less worthy.

- Marriage is a commitment.
- Parenthood is a commitment.
- Watching your favorite TV show each week is a commitment.
- Brushing your teeth each day is a commitment.
- Worshipping the Lord on Sunday morning is a commitment.

It is not commitment that is the problem. We all make commitments. The question is if we are committed to the right things. This week, our final week of 40 Things NOT to Give up for Lent, we will examine the theme of commitment and our commitment to the One who is most worthy of our commitment.

- **Monday:** Worship
- **Tuesday:** Anger
- **Wednesday:** Sacrifice
- **Maundy Thursday:** Community
- **Good Friday:** Grief
- **Holy Saturday:** Joy

35.Worship

Holy Week: Monday

*"The twenty-four elders fall down before him
who is seated on the throne and worship him who
lives forever and ever. They cast their crowns
before the throne, saying, "Worthy are you, our
Lord and God, to receive glory and honor and
power, for you created all things, and by your will
they existed and were created."*
(Revelation 4:10–11, ESV)

Worship is about assigning worth and value. We
worship what we assign the highest value. What some
people value most is their work. The altar at which they
worship is their desk. Other people may value
entertainment. They may worship at the altar of their
TV. What do you give your time, your attention, and
your money? You can tell much about what you worship
by opening up your checkbook and looking at your
calendar.

What is worthy of your money? What is worthy of your
time? You make sacrifices every day. You may sacrifice
a purchase of a new phone because you value more
paying your mortgage. You may sacrifice attending

church on Sunday morning because you value more
your kid's soccer game. We find the money and the time
for the things that we value most.

In Revelation, we have the picture of the 24 elders.
These represent God's Old Testament people (the 12
tribes of Israel) and the God's New Testament people
(the 12 Apostles). They cast their crowns before the
throne. The crowns represent their authority, wealth,
and position. They give all of it away in a gesture that
shows that the One who sits upon the throne is most
worthy of everything. They sacrifice their crowns for
something greater.

Worship involves cost. What does it cost you to
worship? As Americans, our worship is often something
that is done out of convenience. The idea of sacrifice is
lost to many of us. This goes beyond Sunday morning. It
is ultimately about following Jesus. Can you identify a
specific sacrifice in your life because you
follow/worship Jesus? The worship described in
Romans 12:1. It says:

> *"I appeal to you therefore, brothers, by the*
> *mercies of God, to present your bodies as a living*
> *sacrifice, holy and acceptable to God, which is*
> *your spiritual worship." (Romans 12:1, ESV)*

This verse points to denying ourselves for the glory of
someone greater. But when we lose everything, we gain
something more. Jesus says it best:

> *"For whoever would save his life will lose it, but*
> *whoever loses his life for my sake will find it."*
> *(Matthew 16:25, ESV)*

Reflection

1. Evaluate your calendar and your checkbook. What does it show that you value most?

2. What have you sacrificed to follow Jesus?

3. Why is Jesus of most worth?

36.Anger

Holy Week: Tuesday

"Let love be genuine. Abhor what is evil; hold fast to what is good." (Romans 12:9, ESV)

Anger might be a strange thing to NOT give up for Lent. Anger seems like it should be something that we would want to let go. But let me make a case for anger.

This week is Holy Week. When Jesus came into the Temple on Palm Sunday, John says that he braided a whip (see John 2:15). I could almost imagine the rage that Jesus had has he prepared to cleanse the temple. His actions were calculated and came out of righteous anger.

Another incident is when the little children came to Jesus. The disciples rebuked the people bringing the children. Mark tells us that Jesus became indignant towards his disciples (see Mark 10:14). We imagine the picture of this situation with the happy Jesus and the kids sitting on his lap. We don't often think about his reaction to the disciples.

A third instance is when Jesus tells Peter, "Get behind me Satan" (see Matthew 16:23). This is not the nice and safe Sunday School Jesus. I imagine this as the sternest of rebukes that came from Jesus.

Throughout the Old Testament, we see the anger of God stirred. We know that God is holy and righteous. He is without sin. But the Bible also speaks about God being angry.

Anger in itself is not sinful. It is what we do with the anger and where we direct our anger that makes it sinful.

Anger can be a good thing. Romans 12:9 tells us to abhor what is evil. It should anger us that people go hungry. The violence that we see in the streets of our cities and many places in this world ought to bring about anger. It should upset us that bullying is an overwhelming problem in our schools. There is much that is not right in our world. And we should not be okay with that.

Be angry and fight! But fight for what is right. Fight for peace. Fight for justice. Fight for those who are marginalized. Fight for those who cannot fight for themselves. Stand up for those who have no voice. Help those who cannot help themselves.

A final word about anger. Consider the words of Paul in Ephesians:

> *"Be angry and do not sin; do not let the sun go down on your anger, and give no opportunity to the devil." (Ephesians 4:26–27, ESV)*

Notice he says to be angry. But he is also quick to point out that we should not allow our anger to control us.

Rather we are to control our anger. Anger is trumped by love. Often love is expressed through anger. But love should always guide our anger – not the other way around. Consider that we are called to love even those with whom we may be angry.

Reflection

1. Do you think that anger is a sin?

2. What is an example of righteous anger?

3. Where is God calling you, out of love, to have less tolerance for someone's actions?

37.Sacrifice

Holy Week: Wednesday

"Greater love has no one than this, that someone lay down his life for his friends." (John 15:13, ESV)

On Monday, we talked about the tie between worship and sacrifice. Jesus says that there is no greater love than one who would lay down his life for his friends. There is no one who personifies this more than Jesus himself.

Today, I write this out of gratitude. I write in gratitude of my Savior who gave his life for me. He endured the cross, scorning its shame, so that I might be saved from my sin. He took the pain and the punishment that I deserved and made it his own. Thank you, Jesus, for the tremendous gift of salvation.

I also think about the many others who have given their lives. We look to those who have served our country. There are those who died on the battlefield. There are also those who live everyday with the physical and emotional scars of war. Their sacrifices secured the freedom that we enjoy this day. We salute them.

I am also grateful for those who continue to put their life on the line every day. There are the first responders. There is law enforcement. We are thankful for what they do that enables us to live in relative peace, safety, and security.

I also am reminded of the persecuted church. There are many who have faced martyrdom throughout the centuries as a result of their confession of faith. And this is still a present reality for many Christians in many parts of the world. We are grateful for their steadfastness in the face of death. Hebrews 11 describes these people:

> *"Some were tortured, refusing to accept release, so that they might rise again to a better life. Others suffered mocking and flogging, and even chains and imprisonment. They were stoned, they were sawn in two, they were killed with the sword. They went about in skins of sheep and goats, destitute, afflicted, mistreated— of whom the world was not worthy—wandering about in deserts and mountains, and in dens and caves of the earth." (Hebrews 11:35–38, ESV)*

Our prayer is that God would keep those who suffer persecution strong in faith. We pray that their suffering would serve as a witness even to their persecutors. And we pray that we would have the faith and resolve to endure persecution and martyrdom if that fate would befall us. Finally, we give thanks to God for the crown of righteousness and the reward that is given to all who suffer for the sake of the gospel.

Reflection

Lord, thank you for your sacrifice on the cross. Thank you for the many who have made sacrifices to give us a better life. We lift up the persecuted church and those who put their life on the line to follow you. Keep them strong in their confession of faith. Give them endurance. May their witness serve to create and build faith in others. Keep us strong in our faith that we might endure persecution if that day should come. May all of us who live by faith long for the day when we will join you in glory and victory. Amen.

38.Community

Maundy Thursday

"Not neglecting to meet together, as is the habit of some, but encouraging one another, and all the more as you see the Day drawing near."
(Hebrews 10:25, ESV)

Faith is not lived in a vacuum. God has called us to life together. The redemption that Jesus won on the cross was so that we would be reconciled with God. It was also so that we could be reconciled with one another and live in harmony.

The community that God calls us to is the Church. The Church is not a building. It is not an event we attend. The Church is the assembly of God's people. The New Testament Greek word for church is translated "gathering."

We are called to fellowship. But fellowship is something that is terribly misunderstood in the church. We have "fellowship events." This might be going to a church night at the local minor league ballpark. It might be the church bowling league. It might be a potluck dinner. These are good things to do and are part of what it means to be in fellowship, but there is more that makes fellowship.

There are two parts to that word. There is "fellow" and there is "ship." I want you to picture a ship. There are people on the ship. All the people in the boat are going to the same place. That is the idea of fellowship. We are fellows in a ship that share a common destination. If the ship should sink, we will all sink. If the ship should arrive at the port, we will all arrive at the port.

A Christian without a church is like a sailor without a ship. The sailor will not get far without a boat with other sailors. We are working together to reach a common destination. God does not call us to go alone. We get there together. And it is important to recognize that it is more about the journey and the people we share the journey with than it is about the destination.

You are part of something bigger than yourself

It's not about YOU! It's about Jesus. Jesus is glorified when his people do life together in unity and love. I think about the old Sunday School song where we sang, "They Will Know We Are Christians by Our Love."

Keep in mind the church is not perfect. It is flawed. Sometimes deeply flawed! There will be times when we disappoint each other. But that is the opportunity for us to practice grace and forgiveness. It is the opportunity to show that God's mercy and grace have truly entered into our lives.

This is Maundy Thursday. On this night, Jesus instituted the Lord's Supper. Another name for this meal is communion. What joins us together is the forgiveness Jesus won on the cross. It's bigger than any one of us, and we are joining into that when we participate in this meal.

Another big reason God calls us to community is because we can do more together than we can do alone. I have limited time and ability. But when we combine our time and different abilities together, the effort is multiplied.

Reflection

1. Why is living in community hard?

2. Do you think you can live as a faithful Christian outside the church?

3. What kingdom effort can you join together with others for the common good?

39.Grief

Good Friday

"For godly grief produces a repentance that leads to salvation without regret, whereas worldly grief produces death." (2 Corinthians 7:10, ESV)

"Good grief!" That was one of Charlie Brown's favorite lines. But what is so good about grief? How can we put those two words together?

It is good to shed a tear. Grief is necessary. Grief is a process through which we confront our most difficult losses in life. Don't let anyone tell you that you should not grieve. Loss is real. The Bible tells us that even Jesus wept (see John 11:35). We need grief mixed with hope to confront the darkest realities and consequences of sin.

But through it all, for those of us who are believers, we grieve with hope, knowing that Jesus lives and the victory is ultimately won (see 1 Thessalonians 4:13). Grief needs hope. Without hope, grief becomes despair. But grief mixed with hope is an extremely healthy response to the realities of life and death.

Grief points us to our need for a Savior. I shared in a previous lesson that one of the things that I often say at funerals is that death is a fate we will all face. One day we will be the one in the casket with our friends and family members gathered for our funeral. That is sad. But it is that grief that will also draw us to Jesus the Savior who gives us hope.

Today is Good Friday. We might ask what is so good about this Friday? It is the day which Jesus died on the cross. Why would we call it good?

It is good because it is for our forgiveness. It is for our salvation. It is good in that the ultimate act of love and grace was played out on this day. It is a day of mercy. It is a day filled with hope because we know that Sunday is coming.

On this day, the followers of Jesus were grieved over his death. This was the one they had dedicated their lives to follow. This was the one in whom they had placed their hope. The combination of grief plus the loss of hope led to despair. That is not a place they wanted to be. Grief is good, but despair is not.

Grief + loss of hope = despair

Today, we are grieved that Jesus had to die for our sins. But we are at a much different place than the disciples. We see the death of Jesus in the light of the resurrection. We know it was not the nails that held him to the cross. It was his great love for us. We observe the events of the cross with hope. Grief mixed with hope produces a much different result.

Grief + hope = trust in Jesus

Grief and hope will open the door for the 40th (and final) thing NOT to give up for Lent which we will share tomorrow.

Reflection

1. Do you think that grief is good?

2. What does Good Friday mean to you?

3. How is grief different with hope and without hope?

40.Joy

Holy Saturday

"Rejoice in the Lord always; again I will say, rejoice." (Philippians 4:4, ESV)

Rejoice Always

We are almost there. Today is the last day of Lent. We have been preparing for this moment for the last 40 days. Tomorrow is Easter. Easter is the day we celebrate the resurrection. It is a day that is marked with joy and celebration. But this joy is not to be reserved for one day of the year. Jesus is alive every day.

The Apostle Paul tells us to rejoice in the Lord ALWAYS. The most remarkable thing about this verse was that Paul wrote this verse from prison. The prisons of the ancient world were terrible places to be. There are few worse places where Paul might have found himself. But even in these terrible conditions, Paul says: "Rejoice!"

Joy is a mindset. It is more than an emotion. Happiness is an emotion. Happiness is based on circumstances. Joy is not. I can be unhappy and still have joy. Joy is a supreme confidence that comes from God no matter what circumstance I might face.

If all I ever pursued was what made me happy, I would live a miserable life. The things that are good for me are not necessarily what makes me happy in a given moment. The pursuit of fleeting happiness will rob me of lasting joy. Discipline does not make me happy. But there is joy that is derived from living a disciplined life.

I am certain the cross did not make Jesus happy. But we are told that it was for the JOY set before him, that he endured the cross (see Hebrews 12:2). He was not living for happiness but living for joy. The joy was salvation for you and me and eternity together with him.

Surprised by Joy

The story of Easter is such a great story because it is so unexpected. The women that come to the tomb did not discover what they thought they would see. They expected to find a dead body hidden in a cave. What they discovered was that Jesus was alive. It was more than they could have hoped or imagined.

This is the point. God is full of surprises. A life in Christ is filled with unexpected surprises that bring amazing joy. We never know the doors that God will open up and the stones he will roll away when a life is lived in faith.

I leave you with the words of the Apostle Paul in Ephesians 3:14. It is my prayer for you:

> *"For this reason I bow my knees before the Father, from whom every family in heaven and on earth is named, that according to the riches of his*

glory he may grant you to be strengthened with power through his Spirit in your inner being, so that Christ may dwell in your hearts through faith—that you, being rooted and grounded in love, may have strength to comprehend with all the saints what is the breadth and length and height and depth, and to know the love of Christ that surpasses knowledge, that you may be filled with all the fullness of God."
(Ephesians 3:14–19, ESV)

May you experience greater things in God and be filled with immeasurable Easter joy!

Reflection

1. How would you describe the difference between happiness and joy?

2. Where do you find joy? How do you make your aim joy rather than happiness?

3. How do you share joy with others?

4. Celebrate the resurrection! It is our hope and joy.

Bonus: He is Risen!

Easter Sunday

"Now after the Sabbath, toward the dawn of the first day of the week, Mary Magdalene and the other Mary went to see the tomb."
(Matthew 28:1, ESV)

He is risen! He is risen indeed! Alleluia!

This is our triumphant day. Light has dawned. The Son is risen. The tomb is empty. Nothing is impossible with God. He is full of surprises. He has greater things in store for you. The resurrection makes all the difference. Because Jesus lives, you too can live a new and transformed life.

Before light had dawned, the women went to the tomb. They expected to find the dead body of Jesus. The darkness was overwhelming. There were sorrow and tears. Death had won. Hope was lost.

Maybe you can relate to the women as they walked this dark path. Maybe you feel hopeless at this moment. You don't see a future. You wonder where God is. You cannot see anything good.

These women could not have imagined what was about to happen. The sunrise would bring about the Sonrise! It's always the darkest just before the dawn.

Here is what you need to know: Today is a new day. Today is not yesterday. God is up to something. You just never know. He's got a plan that is more than you could ever imagine. Easter is for you!

You may be at your lowest. You may think it's your greatest defeat. But all that means is that the greater God's victory will be. Light is dawning. There is a resurrection coming your way!

Thank you for joining me on this journey during the 40 Days of Lent. It is my prayer that this devotional guide has been a blessing to you. I pray that your observance of Lent has led to an even greater Easter joy.

If you found this resource to be valuable, make sure to visit my website and join my mailing list at:

philressler.com

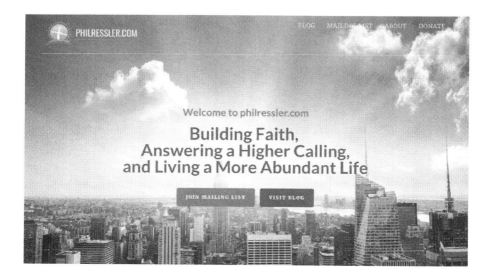

Get my other book!
40 Things to Give up for Lent

Available at Amazon, Barnes & Noble, and on iTunes.

Have you ever wondered what to give up for Lent? Join us on this 40 day adventure through the season of Lent. Each day you will make a new discovery of something truly worth giving up. These 40 things are worth giving up not just for Lent, but for the rest of your life. You can give up things you eat and drink such as soda and chocolate. You can give up bad habits such as smoking or staying up late. But in this devotion you will look at giving up things which will transform your life. You will give up things like bitterness, loneliness, envy, and more. 40 Things to Give up for Lent is a powerful journey that will take your observance of Lent from ordinary to extraordinary.